GUIDED
TAROT

GUIDED TAROT

A Beginner's Guide to Card Meanings, Spreads, and Intuitive Exercises for Seamless Readings

· ·

STEFANIE CAPONI

ZEITGEIST · NEW YORK

Published in the United States by Zeitgeist,
an imprint of Zeitgeist™, a division of
Penguin Random House LLC, New York.

penguinrandomhouse.com

Zeitgeist™ is a trademark of Penguin Random House LLC

ISBN: 9780593196991
Ebook ISBN: 9780593196984

Original illustrations by Pamela Colman Smith
with guidance from Arthur Edward Waite,
first published by William Rider & Son, London, in 1909.

Book design by Aimee Fleck

Printed in China

8th Printing

First Edition

Contents

INTRODUCTION

I was just a teen when I got my first tarot deck, a copy of the Rider Waite Smith. It was the only deck offered in the small metaphysical section of my local bookstore. While I didn't know anyone who was a tarot reader, I found myself drawn to the cards. I had had my eye on them for a while, and after I saved up enough babysitting money, I was able to buy the deck and call it mine. But as it was the pre-internet era, I did not know who to ask about these mysterious cards, so I spent hours with the cards spread out on my bedroom floor, admiring the artwork and poring over the cryptic little book that came with them.

Fast-forward 20 years: I found myself in the wrong career, wrong marriage, and feeling blocked emotionally and creatively. So many questions swirled in my head. How could I have been so out of alignment with what I wanted for such a long time? How could I learn to trust my intuition and guide myself back onto the right path? It was at this crucial time that I returned to and rebuilt my relationship with the tarot. In the days after I ended my marriage, I pulled a three-card spread, and those cards nearly flew out of the deck at me—Death, the Nine of Swords, and, to my surprise, the Magician. The Magician became my inspiration as I developed my intuitive inner guide and let it lead me on an incredible journey of self-discovery. More than 20 years after I'd first picked up a deck, tarot taught me how to honor my higher self and celebrate my own unique gifts. It became central to my life. I started as a student, then evolved into a teacher and created my own tarot deck, *The Moon Void Tarot*, along with its accompanying guidebook. It was a way to help others who were experiencing similar life-altering journeys to communicate with the divine and create new aligned realities.

I believe that each of us holds gifts deep within, from a higher source—and we have the power to unlock those gifts. Tarot is a tool that can help us make those transformative discoveries. The relationship you form with your tarot practice will allow you to connect to your higher self and higher source—whether you call it the divine, god, universe, or something else is entirely up to you. Tarot is spiritual, not religious, and offers its help to anyone and everyone who seeks it out.

With this book, my intention is to assist you in becoming comfortable reading tarot seamlessly and with ease. I would have loved to have a book like this at the beginning of my own tarot journey! I know that it felt daunting when I was first learning the cards— all 78 of them. What makes this book different from other beginning tarot guides is that it includes exercises that are designed to help nurture and grow your intuition and relationship to tarot. Like exercising your muscles at the gym, you will develop and strengthen your intuition as you continually engage in your tarot practice.

This book draws examples from the widely popular Rider Waite Smith deck—the same deck that started my own tarot journey—but you can use any deck of your choosing. We will focus on the universal meanings of each card as well as using your intuition to channel your own meanings rather than memorizing what each card means. I also recommend that you have a journal to record your exercises and intuitive messages as you work with this book. Reading tarot is a custom blend of knowing the cards, listening to your heart, and trusting your own intuition for guidance. This combination allows the cards to communicate ideas and insights that are uniquely and exclusively for you.

I'm honored to share my tarot knowledge and provide this book as a guide to support you along your tarot journey. I encourage you to take your time reading through the pages and pausing to complete exercises, as well as looking at and holding the cards in your hands. As you progress through the book, you might be surprised by how quickly you begin to understand the cards while also learning more about yourself in the process. Soon enough, you'll be confident in doing readings for yourself and even your friends. So grab your deck, and let's begin!

CHAPTER 1

Understanding Tarot

....

GETTING STARTED WITH
tarot is exciting! It can feel like
learning a new language that
connects you with the entire universe.
But before you start shuffling your
deck and pulling cards, let's go
over the basics, including a brief
history of tarot, the structure of
the deck, and how to cleanse and
attune to your deck. We'll also cover
important questions like how to work
responsibly with the tarot, and why
tarot is meaningful in your own life.

....

HOW THE TAROT WORKS

Tarot is more than just an illustrated deck of playing cards to be used for entertainment; when used intentionally, it becomes a conduit. The deck itself takes on a deeply personal meaning when infused with the energy of the individual working with it. It can be an important tool for self-discovery and for deepening your spiritual knowledge. Think of it as a communication device that connects you to the divine—and you can connect anytime! For me, tarot has been a safe support system that's allowed me to look into my past while simultaneously helping me manifest the life of my dreams. It's also helped me become more aware of my internal and external needs. By cultivating a strong connection to myself, I'm able to attract more meaningful relationships and opportunities.

One thing tarot does not do is predict, or tell, the future. Rather, tarot offers confirmation of your intuition, which then empowers you to move forward in life in a way that speaks to your truth and aligns with your purpose. Building a responsible tarot practice means learning to ask productive questions during your readings, then using your intuition to interpret the messages you receive and maintaining awareness of the energy surrounding your situation, so you are able to assist yourself and others in making informed decisions that lead to aligned actions. Sometimes you may not get the answer you wanted to hear, as tarot often points to the areas that need attention in order to reach a desirable outcome. Try to remain flexible and open. The answers to many of life's questions aren't black and white, so don't expect your deck to offer a yes or no response. Instead, trust your intuition; it will be your best asset for interpreting the cards. Notice how you feel and what comes to mind when you see the card's imagery, and allow that reaction to determine if you're on the right track or if you need to do some readjusting.

IT'S IN THE CARDS

Most tarot decks contain a total of 78 cards—22 trump cards called the Major Arcana and 56 cards called the Minor Arcana. The word "arcana" is derived from the Latin root *arcanus*, meaning "secret," and refers to a mysterious or specialized body of knowledge that only a select few people possess. As you can likely guess, the Major Arcana cards hold more significance than the Minor Arcana cards. Some modern decks have extra cards designed by the creator, but in this book, we will be dealing specifically with the classic 78 Major and Minor Arcana.

When the Rider Waite Smith deck was created, it followed the gender conformity of the times. This book therefore uses she/he pronouns to describe the figures shown based on the presentation of the work created in 1909, but it does not reflect the modern fluidity of individual gender identity.

MAJOR ARCANA

The 22 cards that make up the Major Arcana represent significant life events. Cards 0 to 21 take you on a journey, showing you the energy present on both internal and external levels, individually and collectively.

MINOR ARCANA

The remaining 56 cards that make up the Minor Arcana represent everyday influences in your life. While these energies may be less significant, they are the threads that weave our lives together, assisting us in making decisions and getting to know ourselves better. There are four elemental suits that make up the Minors: Cups, Wands, Swords, and Pentacles. Each of the suits contains 10 numbered cards, Ace through 10.

COURT CARDS

Each suit within the Minor Arcana also contains four court cards, much like a deck of playing cards. These cards represent the next level of energy within their respective suits, meaning they are considered masters of their suit and more powerful than the numbered cards. Each of the court cards have already faced the lessons depicted in the Ace through 10 cards and carry that wisdom and experience within them. The Page, Knight, Queen, and King all have their own levels of maturity and talents, giving them more weight than the numbered minors. We will explore the double elements of the court cards over the following chapters. Sometimes they will represent a specific person, an aspect of yourself, or an energy surrounding a situation.

Your Relationship with the Tarot

During my early experiences with my tarot practice, I had many questions—and answering those questions helped develop my relationship with the tarot. I was amazed to see how confrontational yet supportive the answers I uncovered turned out to be, as though I was making important progress in getting to know myself better. Asking and answering questions allowed me to get in touch with myself on a deeper level and to cultivate my spirituality. Curiosity replaced judgment, old wounds became healed, fear melted into love, and life blossomed. Likewise, your relationship with the tarot has the potential to develop into something very profound and meaningful.

As you embark on this journey, take a moment to reflect in your journal. Think about your intentions for your tarot practice. Consider the following prompts, and free-write everything that comes to mind. There are no right or wrong answers.

→   What would I like to gain from my experience with tarot?

→   Which areas of life would I like to improve upon by using tarot?

→   What issues or challenges would I like to leave behind using the assistance of tarot?

→   What is my relationship to my intuition at this moment?

→   What does spirituality mean for me at this time?

Hopefully, after you've taken some time to write in your journal, you'll have some clarity on your intentions. I encourage you to revisit these questions at various stages, even pulling a tarot card to answer each question and recording the messages you receive. Notice how your answers evolve alongside your tarot practice as a means of tracking your inner growth.

BRIEF HISTORY OF THE TAROT

Tarot has been around for more than 600 years! Throughout those six centuries, its meanings and usage have evolved. In the 1400s, a version of the tarot cards featuring four suits, court cards, and trump cards—similar to a traditional deck of playing cards—popped up in various parts of Europe. In the 1800s, tarot cards were being used as divination tools in occult practices, which is likely the source of the belief that tarot is a tool of evil. The Rider Waite Smith deck was drawn by illustrator Pamela Colman Smith from instructions given by academic and mystic A. E. Waite and was published by the Rider Company in 1909. To this day, this deck has the most iconic and recognizable tarot imagery in the world. While the Rider Waite Smith deck uses Judeo-Christian imagery, the symbolism transcends any religious connotations and has inspired most decks released over the last century.

Tarot has increased in popularity over the past decade, largely due to curiosity around spirituality and self-healing, and understanding the law of attraction. A perfect tool for self-discovery and making changes in your life, it helps you co-create with the universe rather than leaving life up to chance.

You do not need to be well versed in the esoteric history of tarot to begin your tarot practice. If you are interested in learning more about the historical, occult, and religious symbolism of these cards, see Resources, page 234.

CHOOSING YOUR DECK

Even though this book uses examples from the Rider Waite Smith deck, that doesn't mean you must use the same deck yourself. (I recognize that it is not an inclusive deck, as it features illustrations of only white-presenting, cisgender characters.) Choosing a deck is a very personal decision, and the deck you pick should reflect your personal preferences. There are many decks to choose from, varying wildly in artistic styles and content. For example, some decks have imagery with lots of people, some have no people, and others may have a single character that appears throughout.

Consider which styles of art speak to you. Do you love color, or are you drawn to black and white? Do you respond to intricate detailed illustrations, or clean and simple imagery? Do you prefer traditional, classic, or very modern? Make sure you choose a deck that has artwork that excites you and makes your experiences feel represented. You will spend quite a bit of time with your tarot deck, so it should feel like a friend or an extension of yourself. (For a comprehensive list of deck suggestions, refer to the references section at the end of this book.)

You may have come across the notion that it is bad luck to purchase your own tarot deck—that a tarot deck should be a gift received from someone else. This is merely a superstition, so don't let it discourage you. Buying your own deck does not diminish your experience. Selecting and obtaining your deck is a power move, so don't wait for the universe to drop one in your lap.

PURIFYING YOUR DECK

The ritual of purifying the deck is an important step. Purifying helps clear any energy that may be attached to the deck before you begin to work with it. It helps you attune to your deck, merging your energy with that of the deck itself to form a bond. You'll want to purify the deck right after you've purchased it and also make a habit of clearing it both before and after you perform readings.

Purification can be done through several methods, so you can choose one that resonates with you. You can record the purifying steps you try and journal about how you felt during the process.

SMOKE

Light an ethically sourced incense, such as mugwort or palo santo, and pass your deck through the smoke a few times, or until it feels clear of any energy previously attached to it. This can be done before and after readings.

CRYSTALS

Clear quartz can effectively remove any superfluous energy to purify your deck. Simply place a crystal on top of your deck before and after use. You may choose to leave your crystal on top of the deck while you store it to purify its energy, or place your crystal on top of the deck for several minutes right before using and right before putting your deck away. You can also use black tourmaline to clear negative energy in the same manner. Make sure the crystals you're using get their own purifying treatment from time to time! You can do this by placing them in a bowl of salt or under a new or full moon monthly.

Interviewing Your Deck

After you have purified your deck, it's time to interview it. This practice of getting to know each card will help you further your bond with the deck. Start by shuffling the cards to help you attune your energy with your deck. (For more details on how to do this, see page 20). Then spread out all of the cards in front of you or go card by card through the deck, taking in the imagery. As you look at each card, you'll notice that certain ones jump right out to you.

Now, grab your journal and ask your deck the following interview questions. Pull a card as the response to each question, taking a few moments to journal about what automatically comes to mind when you see the card.

→ What work are we meant to do together?

→ What are you here to teach me about myself?

→ What are you here to teach me about the world?

→ What card best describes you as a deck?

→ What card best describes me at this time?

Based on the cards you pulled and your responses to these questions, set an intention for your tarot practice. An intention is a positive statement that often begins with "I am" or "I have" and declares what you want. For example, "I am deeply connected to my intuitive powers" and "I have unlimited access to my own inner knowledge" are two intentions that positively proclaim what you want as if it is already yours. Write down your intention in your journal and refer back to it frequently, noticing the shift once it becomes true.

MOONLIGHT

Placing your deck on your windowsill or outside in the moonlight is a powerful way to recharge and purify your deck each month. This can be done during the full or new moon. You can choose to leave your deck in the moonlight overnight or for a couple of hours. The moon's energy is potent; pick the timing that feels right for you to connect to its energy.

BREATH OF LIFE

Don't underestimate the power of your breath! It can be used to purify and clear your deck. Take two to three deep inhalations into your belly and exhale from your mouth directly onto your deck before or after readings to clear the energy.

KNOCKING

Using your knuckles, knock on the top of the deck twice. The vibration and sound emitted are attuned to your personal energetic frequency and effectively clear and purify your deck.

THE CARDS AND THE POWER OF INTUITION

The tarot is an incredible tool for distinguishing between two different internal reactions—one is intuition, which is composed of gut feelings and inner knowledge experienced somatically (meaning in your body); the other is ego, which is composed of thoughts and urges that come from your mind and focus on keeping you safe. These two reactions sometimes clash. Your intuition may be overpowered by your ego's attempts to keep you inside your comfort zone.

The mind and ego want security and concrete answers; memorizing a prescribed meaning for each card satisfies this need. Although there is value in knowing and calling upon the traditional meanings of the cards, tarot is a rewarding and safe way to practice building your intuition, and intuitive readings are often more revealing. The exercises in this book will help you strengthen your intuition, gently allowing your ego to relax and let your inner knowledge shine through. The more you practice allowing your intuition to guide you toward the meanings of the cards, the stronger your intuition will become. And over time, you will learn to perform readings in a way that balances your knowledge of the cards' prescribed meanings and the intuitive meanings that surface as part of each unique reading session.

DESIGNING YOUR OWN DECK

Designing your own deck is an incredible way to strengthen your personal relationship with tarot. You can use a variety of media, and no artistic skills are necessary! Collage is a fun, accessible way to create a deck from scratch. Experiment with color, text, and shapes. The Major Arcana cards are often a good starting point. Consider the energy of each card, one at a time, as you gather images and words to create the essence of the card or what it means to you. Infusing your story into your cards can be a profoundly healing and instructional process.

When I made my first deck, *The Moon Void Tarot*, I made it only for myself, depicting myself as The Fool, with my eyes closed walking with only a wand in hand, topped with a crescent moon, signifying my journey into the unknown, using my intuition as my guide. It is an autobiographical deck. Using myself as the single unifying character, embodying each archetype of the Major Arcana, helped me understand and strengthen my intuition as well as my knowledge of each card. Being specific to my own life experience is deeply cathartic and taught me just how resilient and brave I am.

If you are not ready to create an entire deck, I'd encourage you to start by creating just one card. Trace the outline of a card in your journal, then choose one of your favorite cards. Inside the outline, sketch or write words that embody the card's meaning for you. For example, if I were channeling my inner Queen of Wands, I'd write words like "fiery," "inspired," "energetic," "fierce," and "boss witch." This kind of playful creativity can enhance intuition and relieve stress.

CHAPTER 2

How to Do a Reading

· ·

DON'T LET BEING a beginner psych you out. Everyone can perform tarot readings! In fact, the act of doing your first reading is tied to the symbolism of the deck itself. All of the cards within a tarot deck are involved in the story together, and the foundation of that story is the journey of the Fool, who steps into unknown territory, overcoming fear and self-judgment. That's just what you should do as you dive into the world of readings.

· ·

YOUR ROLE AS A READER

When you do a reading for yourself, it's an exercise in seeing your own situation from an elevated perspective while simultaneously being immersed in your experience. If you are feeling heightened emotions, you can pull a card to engage with that energy. For example, you can ask yourself questions like: What am I most upset about right now? Or how can I calm my mind at this moment? If you feel confused or overwhelmed by what you're feeling, return to your breath to clear your mind. Breathing deeply for two or three breaths, and listening to the sound of the air entering and leaving your body, will help you receive clear and helpful answers.

When reading for someone else, set the intention of removing your personal feelings so that you can more effectively channel messages for your querent (the person for whom you are reading). Your role is to interpret the cards based on their established meanings, combined with intuitive messages that you receive from their imagery during the course of the reading session. Encourage your querent to express any intuitive messages they receive when they look at the cards, but try not to guide them toward a specific answer or direction. Don't take anyone's reactions personally, since you are merely interpreting the cards in front of you. If the querent asks you for guidance on how to proceed, decide how comfortable you are with offering action steps. For example, you can ask your deck for a message regarding the next steps the querent can take to resolve the situation. Pulling an additional card or two can help direct the conversation and assist you and the querent in deciding together what comes after the reading.

PERFORMING A READING

Clear and accurate readings come from following a specific set of steps, including grounding, shuffling, cutting the deck, and laying out the cards in a pattern called a spread. Traditionally, tarot readers choose a specific spread before beginning their readings. The most popular spread is the 10-card Celtic Cross, but simple three-card spreads are perfect for beginners (see Chapter 3, Tarot Spreads, page 32). They're easier to comprehend, and they create a foundation for more complex spreads down the line.

Before you start, take a moment to burn some incense or light a candle, or take a few deep breaths while holding your favorite crystal. There is no right or wrong way to do this; your spiritual practice is your own. The key is to do something that helps you open yourself to channeling clear messages.

STEP 1: GROUNDING

Grounding your energy before you engage your deck allows you to tap into universal energy during your readings. The process of grounding connects your swirling mind to your body, and your body to the earth. Take a few deep breaths to clear your mind; feel your breath fill your entire body, from the top of your head down to your feet. Next, imagine your feet connected to the ground, visualizing roots growing from your feet down into the earth. Come back to the room as you open your eyes and begin your reading. When reading for someone else, invite the querent to join you by breathing together. This attunes you as the reader to the energetic frequency of the querent, so you may channel messages on their behalf.

STEP 2: SHUFFLING THE DECK

Shuffling is the best method to attune your energy with your deck right before a reading. There is no right or wrong way to shuffle, so feel free to experiment until you find your style. If the cards fall on the floor while you shuffle or the entire deck goes flying, that's okay! Just go with it!

When reading for yourself, shuffle the cards until you feel your energy seamlessly blending with the energy of your deck. Continue moving the cards while envisioning the subject of your inquiry, and set your intention to receive clear messages. When reading for someone else, you can either shuffle for them or have the querent shuffle to merge their energy with the cards. I prefer to shuffle for my clients, since I'm confident that I am able to channel their energy through a shared grounding practice, but you may feel differently, especially as you're just getting started.

STEP 3: CUTTING THE DECK

Using your dominant hand (known as the hand of action), you will cut the deck as another way to merge your energy with the cards. This signifies your choice to take action while inviting divine guidance. Once you've shuffled to a comfortable stopping point, cut the deck into two or three even piles using your hand of action. Afterward, stack your piles back into one, still using your hand of action. If you prefer to have your querent interact directly with the cards, they can cut the deck and restack it into one pile.

STEP 4: DRAWING CARDS

When the deck is in one pile, use your nondominant hand (known as the hand of intuition) to select your card or cards. You can hold the cards and fan them out, spread the deck out on the table or floor in front of you, or simply choose from the top of the shuffled pile, but always use your hand of intuition to pull cards. Feel free to experiment and choose the method of drawing that feels most comfortable to you.

STEP 5: LAYING OUT THE CARDS

With the layout you have in mind (see Chapter 3, page 32), you will pull cards for each position in the spread, asking one question at a time (or saying what each position means) either out loud or in your head, then drawing your card and leaving it face down before you move on to the next question. Knowing the position of the cards as you lay them out comes in handy as you begin to work up to more complex spreads, such as the Celtic Cross.

Start off with simpler spreads with three or fewer cards, making sure to keep all cards face down until all of the questions have been asked. This will give you the most accurate reading. If you see a card before asking the next question, its energy informs the following cards drawn and overrides your intuition.

You can also use a significator card in your readings. Rather than a random card pulled from the deck, a significator card is specifically chosen as a guide to assist in the reading. Pull the significator card from the deck and lay it down, face up, while you shuffle the cards. For example, the Lovers can be used as a significator in a spread focused on romance, and Justice can be used as a significator in a spread focused on a legal issue or dispute.

STEP 6: TURNING OVER THE CARDS

There is no right or wrong way. As you turn over each card, take a moment to see and react to the imagery before consulting with its written meaning. If you are reading for yourself, write down your intuitive observations in your journal. If you are reading for someone else, tell them what you are noticing without judging yourself.

STEP 7: INTERPRETING THE CARDS

Once all the cards needed for your chosen spread are laid out in front of you, notice how they look together. Is there a prevalence of one particular suit—Swords, Cups, Pentacles, or Wands? When more than one card of any particular suit appears, it can point to the type of energy dominating your spread. Are the cards upright or reversed? Upright means the image appears as intended, and reversed means the image is upside-down. Depending on the image's orientation, the card will take on a different meaning. For an in-depth look at reading reversals, see page 24.

Are there any Major Arcana cards? If these cards were telling us a story, what would it be? How do their positions in the spread influence their stand-alone meanings as individual cards? Try to create a narrative for the cards yourself before you rely on their written descriptions. For more guidance on interpreting, see How to Interpret the Cards, page 23.

During your readings, you may find yourself forgetting the traditional meanings of certain cards—this is natural! Take a deep breath, relax, and let the imagery on the card speak to you. Trust the words, ideas, and phrases that resonate.

STEP 8: CLEANSING THE DECK

At the end of each reading, I always thank my cards for their messages. Gratitude for your practice is as essential as setting your intention for a reading. Once you've thanked your deck, you may clear the energy of this specific, concluded reading by knocking on top of it twice or by placing a clear crystal on top of it. When reading for someone else, consider using an ethically sourced incense cleanse in addition to your regular energy-cleansing method to remove their energy from your deck.

STEP 9: STORING YOUR DECK

Some readers store their tarot cards in a wooden box or cloth bag; some prefer to put them back in their own box and put them on a shelf, or in a drawer. I have a dedicated shelf for my tarot decks and keep some in their boxes. My most treasured decks are kept in cloth bags with a clear quartz crystal. Protecting the cards from getting bent and torn is the most important part of storage. Consider which items sit near your deck when it's not in use. For example, keeping them in a drawer surrounded by random clutter may not create the best energy for receiving clear messages. Instead, keep them somewhere that inspires you and brings you peace.

HOW TO INTERPRET THE CARDS

As you now know, there are two main ways to read tarot—by understanding their traditional meanings and by following your own intuitive guidance. As we move into the world of interpretation, I want to revisit the importance of both methods of reading.

Each card in the deck is associated with a set of traditional meanings and key terms, with one set for the upright position and one set for the reversed position. Since tarot card images evoke archetypes that have appeared in countless stories throughout human history, these traditional meanings form a common thread that runs through virtually every deck. In this book, we'll focus on these shared, universal meanings rather than diving into detailed historic symbolism. And as you begin to read and interpret, consulting traditional card meanings may help you draw information from your spreads, including how each card's imagery relates to the elemental suits, or the weighted significance of a situation based on numbers of Major or Minor cards drawn.

The intuitive meanings of the cards come through when you allow yourself to channel your feelings and inner knowledge. Feel free to consult the traditional meanings, but never be afraid to express ideas or interpretations that come to you naturally during the course of your readings. The more you allow yourself to voice your own unique interpretations, the stronger your connection to your intuition will become. Try to remember to draw on both knowledge and intuition to create a rich and meaningful reading experience.

No matter which cards you pull, it is important to remember that you (and your querents) have free will over your choices. If the spread tells you something worrisome, you can choose to work with the energy or work toward shifting it.

NARRATIVE READINGS

Doing a narrative reading means looking at the cards together to form a complete story. Try this with smaller spreads, such as three-card pulls. For instance, when you lay out three cards, you can use the traditional keywords associated with each card to construct a sentence. For example, if you selected the Fool, Three of Wands, and Eight of Pentacles, you would get the keywords "new beginning," "expansion," and "fulfilling work." If you string that into a sentence, you may come up with a sentence such as "A new beginning opens you up to expanding your potential to create a more fulfilling career." You can incorporate the intuitive messages you get from each card to expand on your simple sentence as well, allowing them to offer you clues to more profound meanings.

REVERSALS

When you draw a card, you will notice the orientation of the artwork; it will be upright or reversed (upside-down). When a card is drawn with the imagery reversed, it varies in meaning from its upright counterpart. Your intuition plays a big role in determining the message that the card is trying to reveal to you. In the beginning, reading reversals may feel overwhelming. Feel free to read all cards as upright for as long as it takes until you are comfortable incorporating reversals. You can also opt not to read reversals.

In my experience, reversals can have several different meanings, and you can allow your intuition to guide you to their significance within a specific reading session. A reversed tarot card can point to the following:

A WAITING PERIOD The upright energy of the reversed card may not yet be ready for you to integrate fully. It's on its way, but there is something that needs to happen before it arrives and manifests. For example, the reversed Knight of Pentacles could signify a wonderful new job opportunity is forthcoming, but it is taking longer than expected, so be patient and remain optimistic.

A BLOCK TO ITS UPRIGHT MEANING The reversed card can point to an energetic block where the upright energy is concerned. For example, the reversed Ace of Cups could mean that a new relationship is possible, but first you must make sure you are putting your energy into loving yourself and tending to your own needs.

INTERNAL VERSUS EXTERNAL The reversed card may point to something that is happening within you rather than outside of you. For example, the reversed Six of Swords can indicate that you don't feel comfortable talking about your problems or reaching out for support from people who care about you, and this is holding you back.

DIRECTION OF ENERGY Say you are doing a Past, Present & Future reading and the middle card (representing the present) is reversed. Are the figures or symbols shown on that middle card pointing at the past or the future? For example, you may pull the Emperor for the past, Knight of Cups reversed for the present, and Two of Wands for the future. Notice if the reversed Knight appears to be offering the cup to the Emperor in the past position rather than to the Two of Wands in the future. This indicates you may be putting your energy on trying to fix something from the past rather than moving toward a new beginning.

COURT CARDS

Page, Knight, Queen, and King are court cards, or the masters of their suit. As I mentioned in Chapter 1, this means they have already experienced the lessons that begin with Ace and end with Ten. Court cards can be tricky for some people to interpret, since we tend to assign gender to the roles they represent, but when court cards appear in your reading, you can intentionally read them as gender-neutral. Instead of assigning gender, notice the information they yield in regard to their mastery of the elemental suits. Here's a quick rundown:

PAGES are novices with experience that pertains to each specific suit, but they have not yet become the Knight, who goes out to experience the world.

KNIGHTS represent the elemental speed with which events occur (fire burns faster than water flows, etc.). The Knight's quest is to experience each element and attain the next level of mastery.

QUEENS have receptive energy of their suit, nurturing and receiving at a master level that benefits themselves and others in a pure way.

KINGS have active energy of their suit, taking on positions of power and leadership from experience.

Daily Reading

This simple daily reading ritual allows you to work with tarot regularly without overloading yourself with complicated questions and interpretations. In the beginning, you can read every card upright, as this helps to form a solid foundation of knowledge before introducing reversals. Here's how a one-card daily reading could work:

1. Once you've made a cup of coffee or tea, grab your journal and set up your space.

2. Clear the energy from the deck, then take a few deep breaths to clear your mind.

3. As you shuffle, simply ask your cards (silently or out loud): what do I need to know today? Then pull a single card from the deck and give it your full intuitive attention.

4. In your journal, write down your daily card and the thoughts that arise when you see it. What feelings or reactions does the image on the card create for you?

Journaling about your initial thoughts and feelings upon seeing your daily card helps you work with your intuition. Wait until you finish writing everything that comes to mind before looking up the card's traditional meaning. Notice if that meaning is similar to your intuitive messages. Does the traditional meaning of the card build on or contradict what you initially felt? Sometimes the traditional meaning and your intuition contradict each other. In my experience, when that happens it's a signal from your intuition to pay attention to issues in your life linked to that particular card. Trust that each card is the right message for you each day.

NUMEROLOGY

Each card has a number on it, and these numbers can offer additional guidance to their meaning. There may be 22 Major Arcana cards, but in numerology (the study of numbers and their meanings), all multiple-digit numbers are reduced to 1 through 10. For example, to get the numerological meaning for the Sun (card number 19), you'd add 1 + 9 = 10. See the associations for each number below, become familiar with them, and you can add this layer of knowledge to your readings. I've found that remembering the numerological correlations of each card assists me in recalling the traditional meanings of each card without having to look them up. For example, it's helpful for me to remember that the Emperor is associated with the number 4, which connects with structure, stability, and foundation. As a beginner, if this section feels too complicated, skip it for now and come back to it when you feel ready!

1 — The Individual, New Beginning

2 — Choice, Duality, Partnership

3 — Creativity, Collaboration, Community

4 — Structure, Stability, Foundation

5 — Change, Instability, Loss

6 — Balance, Choice, Harmony

7 — Inspired Action, Magic

8 — Infinity, Success, Power

9 — Alone, Near Completion

10 — Completion, End of a Cycle

COMMON QUESTIONS

As a teacher of tarot, I've encountered all kinds of questions from students as well as clients. I've been asked, "Are there dark entities trapped in the cards?" (Nope!) And, "Exactly how many babies will I have?" (Not something tarot can reveal.) I've had students ask how to develop their own style of reading, which deck would suit them best, and more. Here are some examples of the questions that come up frequently:

Q: **What types of questions should I ask the tarot?**

A: Ask productive questions rather than yes, no, when, how, or why questions. If you have trouble with this at first, try reframing your thoughts. For example, instead of "When will I meet my soul mate?" a more productive question would be "What card represents my relationship energy at this time?" or "What can I do to be open and receptive to a healthy romantic relationship?" When asking about money and your career, instead of asking "When will I get a raise?" try more productive questions, such as "How should I focus my energy to increase my income?" or "What hidden potential should I be aware of that will bring new wealth opportunities into my life?"

Q: **Can the cards predict future events?**

A: The cards do not predict the future but rather offer information about the available energy that surrounds a situation. For example, if a querent is asking about a new relationship and you draw the Three of Swords, the energy that is surrounding that situation may still be in the healing stages. The person of interest in this relationship may not be emotionally available quite yet, or the querent may still be recovering from a past heartbreak. Conversely, if you draw the Two of Cups, the energy of mutual connection surrounds your question.

As the cards pick up on your energy, they can offer insight into what is possible, but try not to focus on outcomes exclusively. Instead, use the cards to identify forces in your present reality that can help you move toward the future you'd like to create. Even in a Past, Present & Future reading, the card that represents the future is showing you what is *possible*. Your free will determines how future messages play out.

Focused Readings

As a new reader, it can be challenging to remember the traditional meanings of each card and all facets of its interpretation. Performing focused readings can remove some of that pressure by allowing you to tune into certain specific aspects of the cards. Make sure to record your experiences with focused readings in your tarot journal—what you enjoyed and what you've learned. Know that you can incorporate any of these methods into your tarot practice at any time.

NUMBER READING

This reading asks you to pay attention only to the number on each card and notice how the meaning of the number (see Numerology, page 27) enhances the card's imagery and energy. Without asking any questions, pull three cards. With each card that you pull, see if you can remember what each card's number means. In a spread, you can also add up the value of each card and use that as the overall message of the reading. For example, if you pull the Seven of Pentacles (7), Justice (11), and the Sun (19): $7 + 1 + 1 + 1 + 9 = 10$. Ten means completion or the end of a cycle. You may be thinking, "Great, the end of a cycle . . . but what comes next?!" To answer this, you can take it a step further and make it a single digit, by adding the individual numbers in 10 so that $1 + 0 = 1$. One represents the strength of the individual, meaning you have everything within you to ensure growth and success, and a new beginning is on its way once the current cycle is complete.

COLOR READING

A color reading relies on your intuitive feelings as you relate to the colors on each card. Color can set an emotional tone, so this is a great reading for cultivating your energetic connection with your deck. Again, pull three cards without holding any questions in your mind. As you look at each card, notice its most prominent color. For example, in the Rider Waite Smith deck, the Three of Swords has a melancholy gray background with a bright red heart in the center. How does that make you feel? In your journal, record the colors that jump out immediately to you and the emotions they create.

Q: How do I deliver hard or heartbreaking messages?

A: Before a reading, ask for the querent's consent to deliver any messages that arise, both negative and positive. If an unfavorable message comes through, pull an additional card or two about what can be learned from the situation, or what silver lining is present that can provide comfort during a difficult time.

Q: What if the messages don't make any sense?

A: Take a deep breath—this happens to everyone! If your energy is scattered, the cards can reflect your lack of grounding (or the querent's). After you take a deep breath, pull a clarifying card or two. These additional cards can provide insight into a confusing reading. For instance, if you draw the Queen of Cups as your clarifying card, notice if your intuition guides you to a specific person or emotional experience in your own life. Then you'll know what your initial cards were trying to reveal to you. When performing a reading for yourself, you can always step away from your cards and take some space to journal about the reading. Your writing may lead you to deeper meaning once you've cleared your head.

During a reading for someone else, do not be afraid to enlist the assistance of your querent. Be open and transparent, let them know that the messages appear to be conflicting, and ask them what they are currently experiencing. Most people treat their tarot readings as a spiritual counseling session and are eager to talk about their feelings. Use their words as context for the cards you've pulled. If that still isn't making sense, it's perfectly acceptable to clear your deck and reshuffle! Ground your energy with your querent and begin again. You're just starting out, so don't be hard on yourself; we have all been there.

Q: How do I handle negative cards?

A: Plot twist: there are no negative cards! Cards such as Death, the Devil, and the Nine of Swords can be confrontational, since they are asking us to deal with the less-than-sunny aspects of our lives, but they are not inherently negative or bad. Any card that makes us uncomfortable is pointing to an area of life we find challenging. If we meet these cards with curiosity instead of fear, that creates space for more personal growth and healing.

What Do You See?

You can develop your intuition by studying the imagery on each card and writing down your own interpretations in your journal. Simply free-write your feelings and the messages that arise to anchor the experience. What speaks to you? Is it the colors or specific symbols you see on a particular card? In your journal, write down your intuitive interpretations and feelings. Whatever comes to you is exactly what you're meant to receive, so try not to second-guess yourself.

In the later sections of this book that contain definitions and card meanings, you'll find an additional journal question for you to ask yourself about each card in your deck. Remember that what you see in the cards is just as important as their traditional meanings.

CHAPTER 3

Tarot Spreads

....

NO SUBJECT IS off-limits in tarot,
so allow the spreads to assist you in all
aspects of your journey, from relationships
and finances to spirituality and decision-
making. Most new readers find it easiest
to start with simple spreads as they
familiarize themselves with their decks.
You can begin reading a single card each
day, then gradually build up to two- and
three-card spreads. As your confidence
grows, you can experiment with five-card
spreads and finally work your way up to the
Celtic Cross. It's also worth noting that the
instructions for the more complex spreads
in this chapter assume that you have some
tarot-reading best practices mastered, so if
you skip ahead, those instructions might
feel a bit sparse! All the more reason to
get comfortable with more straightforward
spreads before progressing to the intricate
ones at the end of the chapter.

....

Release & Retain

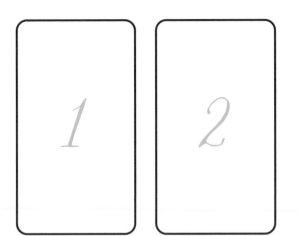

1. RELEASE

What is ready to leave your life or has been taking up too much of your attention and energy?

2. RETAIN

What is necessary to keep for continual growth?

This powerful two-card spread is helpful when you are feeling stuck between relying on old patterns or habits and developing new ones. Letting go can mean something physical, such as a relationship, job, or objects in your home that need to be cleared out to make room for something new that's ready to enter your life. It can also represent nonphysical aspects, such as habitual thoughts and ideas about the way we believe our lives should be.

If a Major Arcana card appears in either position, it represents a significant area of development, whereas a Minor Arcana card shows smaller shifts that can have a great impact. Listen to your inner voice as you observe your initial emotional response to seeing these cards next to one another. In your journal, write down the thoughts that arise along with any other observations.

You have the option to leave the spread as it is or to expand upon the messages by asking these additional questions and pulling one card for each answer.

→   How can I support myself through these changes?

→   What comes on the other side of release?

→   What am I ready to welcome into my life in place of what I'm releasing?

Asset & Hindrance

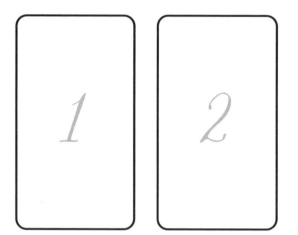

1. ASSET
A natural gift or ability you possess

2. HINDRANCE
Something that may be blocking your gift from manifesting

Tarot can help uncover your natural gifts and assist you in developing them further. This two-card spread focuses on a strength you may not realize you have, and something that may be hindering its discovery. Become curious about your spiritual gifts and open your mind to what you could unearth.

Notice which types of cards are in either position. A Major Arcana card in either position carries more weight than a Minor Arcana card. Observe which elemental suits appear—if there are Swords, Cups, Pentacles, or Wands in both card positions. When more than one card of any particular element appears, it can point to the type of energy dominating your spread. With these things in mind, use your intuition; allow the messages of each card to reveal your gifts and lead you to confront where you may be out of alignment with them. Approach what you receive with curiosity rather than judgment.

You have the option to leave the spread as is or to expand upon the messages it's given you by asking these additional questions and pulling one card for each answer.

→ How can I develop this asset further?

→ What can be done to release what is hindering me?

→ How can I integrate my gifts into my current lifestyle?

Advice from the Universe

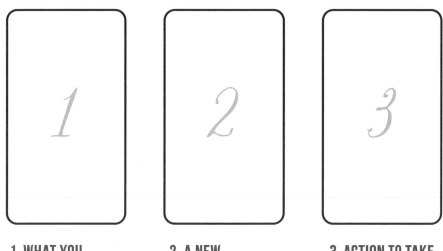

1. WHAT YOU NEED TO KNOW

Something signif-
icant to focus on
about the situation
or topic in mind, or
your life in general

2. A NEW PERSPECTIVE

What you may not be
able to see, allowing
you to expand the
possible ways to
shift this situation

3. ACTION TO TAKE

An actionable step
to take toward a
favorable outcome

This three-card spread can be general or specific. Either set an intention around a topic that's troubling you or simply ask the universe for general guidance when you're feeling unsure. We often become stuck in narrow thinking patterns, and this spread helps us see the opportunities for growth that are always around us.

You can consider each card individually in relation to its position, but this spread is also good for observing cards together as a narrative. What visual story might they be telling? Can you build a sentence that starts with the first card, incorporates the second, and ends with the third? Notice any elements on the cards that jump out immediately. Pay attention to the subtle ways the universe is communicating with you through the cards and their symbolism. As your day goes on, ask the universe to continue to send you messages pertaining to your spread. Observe how your situation begins to shift and expand, and record your experiences in your journal.

Past, Present & Future

| *1* | *2* | *3* |

1. PAST
The energy that is behind you now

2. PRESENT
The energy of your current situation

3. FUTURE
Possible outcome or influence ahead of you

This classic three-card spread is a fantastic tool for energetic check-ins around a particular subject. For example, if you have been working toward a career goal, you can use this spread to see where you were, where you are now, and where you are headed. This spread can be used for any situation, including relationships, personal growth, and living situations, to name a few.

First, look at the card in the past position; is it a Major or Minor Arcana card? Is it upright or reversed? What does your intuition tell you about this card? Does it feel resonant to the situation you were thinking of, or does it point to a factor that you had not considered? Journal about your initial reactions to help tease out this card's significance as needed. Next, look at the present position card, observing and journaling as you did for the past card and following the same steps for the future card.

Finally, look at the three cards together. Using your intuition, allow them to tell a story to you. Do these cards appear to flow? Is a clear theme or message presenting itself? Record your impressions in your journal, and notice if any additional insights come to you throughout the day.

Mind, Body & Spirit

1. MIND

Rational thought as
well as the need for
safety and certainty

2. BODY

What is in your heart,
the emotional intuitive
information you feel
in your physical body

3. SPIRIT

Your connection
to the ethereal
realm, the universe,
and the divine

This spread offers clarity and insight into three core components of your existence—mind, body, and spirit—and the important messages each of them has to offer. Cultivating awareness of the messages coming through each of these channels allows you to learn to work with them, which, in turn, empowers you to bring your best self forward every day.

Knowing the difference between your state of mind (the presence of negative or positive thought patterns) in relation to the emotions that can be felt in your body (gut feelings, uneasiness, excitement, sadness, etc.) is especially helpful when you feel conflicted or confused about a particular subject. The spirit card helps you understand the connections between your physical body's state of being and your soul's higher purpose.

In this spread, observe each card separately in relationship to its position. In your journal, you can record these messages, taking time to explore what comes up for you. Next, view the cards together as a story, taking note of the imagery, colors, and elements of each card. This is a great introductory spread since it encourages learning about yourself by exploring your internal landscape rather than focusing on outward actions.

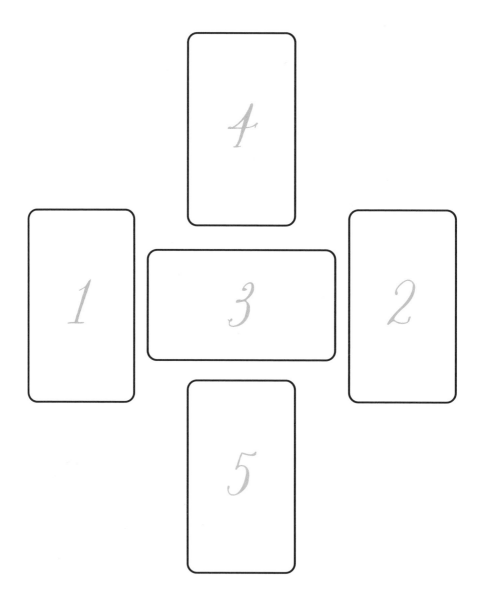

1. ME
Your energy in the relationship

2. THEM
Your partner's energy in the relationship

3. THE BRIDGE
What connects the two of you, for better or worse

4. HIGHEST POTENTIAL
The strongest aspect of the relationship, or an area that needs to be nurtured and strengthened

5. LOWEST POTENTIAL
The weak spot in the relationship, or an area that needs work

Relationships are a popular topic in tarot. When performing a reading that relates to love or relationships, it is important to remember that you cannot control anything or anyone; you can only control your own behavior, feelings, and actions. This spread focuses on the energy that surrounds your current relationship and offers insight into and clarity on areas that can be strengthened or released, depending on the unique circumstances of your situation. This spread can be used for romantic partnerships as well as friendships, family dynamics, and business relationships.

First, look at just the cards that represent you and your partner. What energy exists between the two of you? Does it feel complementary or contradictory? Whatever intuitive messages come up right away, record them in your journal.

Next, look at the third card, which represents the bridge that connects the two of you. Is there something in the imagery that calls to mind a strength, trait, or experience you share that binds you together? If there are two figures in the card's imagery, what are they doing? How does it connect back to your own relationship?

Finally, cards four and five deal with the light and the shadow aspects of the relationship, respectively. This is where work must be done for the relationship to grow and thrive. The fourth card shows you what's strongest right now. How does the symbolism in this card reflect an aspect of your relationship that works well or feels solid? The fifth card illuminates an aspect that needs attention or healing. Look at the figures and symbols in the card's illustration and let your mind make connections. Are there people in the image, or representations of action? How can you connect those back to aspects of your relationship that feel out of alignment?

Your Potential Relationship

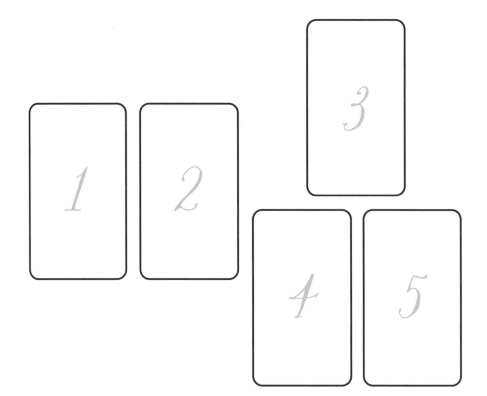

1. ME

Your current relationship energy, or the energy you are emitting around love and relationships

2. WHAT LOVE ASKS OF ME

What is needed to align with the relationship you are seeking

3. MESSAGE FROM THE UNIVERSE

Key information from the universe, your spirit guides, your higher self, or the divine regarding the potential relationship

4. ACTION TO TAKE

An action step you can take to align with the potential relationship

5. WHAT TO RELEASE

A gentle confrontation of something that's taking up too much energetic space and must be released to create room for the relationship to form

Remember that tarot does not predict the future but rather assists you in understanding the energy you bring or need to bring into your life to make certain desired outcomes possible—in this case, focusing on attracting new relationships. Whether you are looking for love or a new job opportunity, or seeking out your soul family/ community, this powerful spread will help you see where growth, action, and release are needed in order to manifest what you desire. It helps you understand where you are in the present moment to inform the energetic potential of new relationships.

Break up the spread by first addressing cards one and two, noticing where you are and what is needed to bring this desired relationship to fruition. The cards will pick up on subtle hidden emotions, such as underlying sadness, anxiety, fear, or readiness and enthusiasm. Card three is a message from the divine regarding your current situation, providing further guidance around what you learned in the previous two cards. Once you have considered the messages from the first three cards, you can look to cards four and five for action and release. Take a moment to journal about these messages, considering the ways you can work within yourself to make internal changes that will lead to manifesting change in your external life.

As always, combine your own interpretations of the cards with their traditional meanings to draw conclusions about this spread's messages. For instance, when you're contemplating card three—the Message from the Universe card—consider the themes, colors, figures, and symbols you see. Which of them seems to represent the divine? What emotions does the image evoke? Ponder on your own first before looking them up.

Law of Attraction

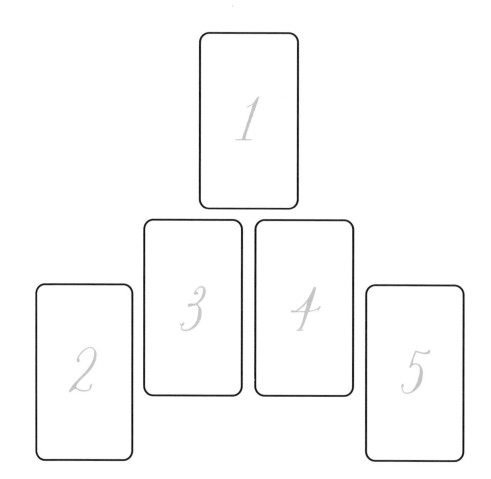

1. SIGNIFICATOR CARD

Choose a card based on your desired manifestation (see page 21)

2. YOUR CURRENT ENERGY

Your current vibrational energy in relation to what you want

3. THE ENERGY YOU NEED

The vibrational match needed to achieve your desires

4. HOW TO GET INTO ALIGNMENT

The internal or external action needed to shift your energy to match your desire

5. LETTING GO OF THE HOW

What you must do to release control of the outcome by staying open to the unlimited number of ways your desire can manifest

Everything and everyone vibrates at a particular energetic frequency, and how you approach situations and interactions reflects your own energy back to you. This powerful spread will help you to see the energy you bring and understand how to shift it to match the energetic frequency of your desires. This spread can be applied to career, finances, romance, community, and good health. Anything you want to attract into your life begins with aligning yourself with its energy.

Begin with the feelings that come up when you see your significator card, which represents your desire, in relation to the card that represents your current energy. Record your intuitive messages in your journal. Card four is the bridge between cards two and three; notice the visual narrative of the three cards together. The energetic journey continues with card five as you use your intuition to guide you in ways of expanding your perspective on the many ways your desire may manifest. You can revisit this spread as a check-in to see how your energetic shift into alignment progresses, journaling as you note any changes.

Making a Decision

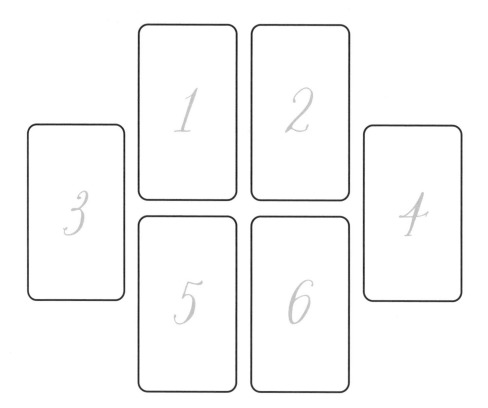

1. OPTION 1
One of the choices within a decision that needs to be made

2. OPTION 2
The other option, which could include the choice to take no action

3. OPTION 1 ENERGY
The energy surrounding the first option

4. OPTION 2 ENERGY
The energy surrounding the second option

5. FEARS
Your fears surrounding change

6. BLESSINGS
The blessings that come from making the decision

We constantly worry about making the right decisions, and that worry can lead to inaction. This helpful spread will show you the energy that is driving your choices so you do not remain stuck or at an impasse. Making a decision will always move you forward. The only wrong choice to be made is making none at all.

Notice the intuitive messages and feelings that arise when you see cards one and two, and record them in your journal. These two cards are mostly symbolic, showing you representations of the choice options themselves. Notice how your deck has chosen to reflect these options back at you. Is there anything that jumps out at you in the images, showing you details of these options you hadn't previously considered?

Next, examine the messages presented by cards three and four in relation to the first two cards. Cards one and two represent the choice options themselves, but cards three and four tell you about the forces behind those options and the reasons that you might be prevaricating or hesitating. Which option does the deck seem to be favoring? Is there any information in the imagery that shows you why one option might be stronger than the other?

The same fears that intuitively come up when you see card five can be applied to both choices, as they are two sides of the same coin. Look to card six to offer insight into the blessings and relief that come from making a decision; your intuition will lead you toward the decision that is right for you.

The Celtic Cross

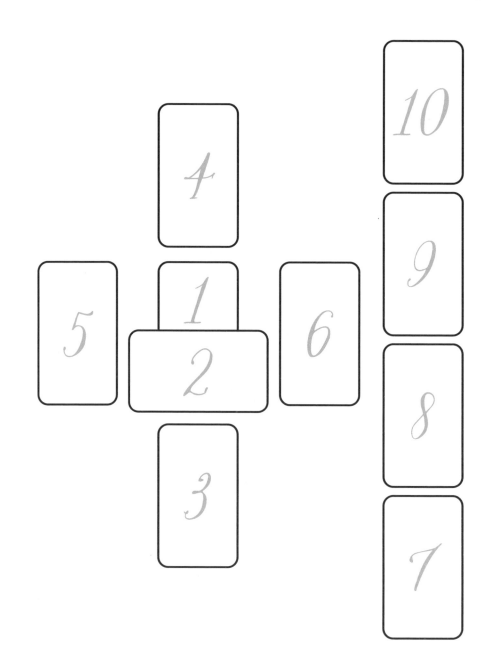

1. CURRENT SITUATION

The energy around your current situation

2. OPPOSING ENERGY

The energy that opposes or blocks your situation

3. WHAT LIES BENEATH

Unconscious forces that affect your situation

4. WHAT IS ABOVE

What you are conscious of regarding your situation

5. WHAT IS BEHIND YOU

Past events that affect your situation

6. WHAT IS BEFORE YOU

Potential events you will face

7. YOUR FEELINGS

Feelings about the situation, or what is in your heart

8. OTHER PEOPLE'S FEELINGS

How others' feelings influence the situation

9. YOUR HOPES OR FEARS

Use your intuition to distinguish whether the card represents your hopes or fears in the situation

10. POTENTIAL OUTCOME

A likely outcome of the situation

This widely popular 10-card spread takes the reader on a journey through the past, present, and future, as well as their internal and external landscape, as they move toward hope for a positive outcome. The Celtic Cross illuminates the forces that affect our lives, including our own thoughts and perceptions of the past, fear of the unknown, and how we let others influence our decisions. It's much easier to understand the messages in the cards by breaking the reading into two parts (see pages 48-49). This allows you to compartmentalize events outside your control, what is in your head, what is in your heart, and what doesn't belong to you.

CONTINUED ▶

The Celtic Cross (cont.)

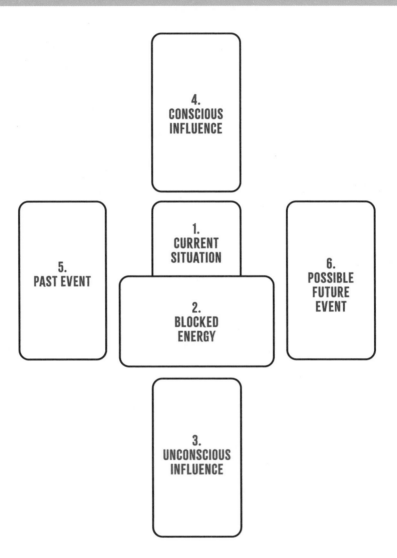

First, look at the body of the cross. Cards one and two are in direct opposition to one another, creating tension. Cards three through six explain more about that tension. Cards three and four show your internal process regarding the situation, while cards five and six point to the external events that are affecting the situation.

10. **POTENTIAL** **OUTCOME**

9. **HOPES** **OR FEARS**

8. **OTHERS'** **OPINIONS** **OR OUTSIDE** **INFLUENCES**

7. **YOUR** **FEELINGS** **(WHAT IS** **IN YOUR** **HEART)**

The remaining four cards represent the ladder we must climb to reach a potential outcome. The ladder consists of our own feelings about the situation and how others' energy affects our reality. Before we reach the top, we must confront our fears and hopes and allow them to drive us toward our goal. (Card nine can represent hopes, fears, or both. If you're not sure which your card is reflecting, try to allow your intuition to guide you toward significant messages.) Finally, we take in the energy that represents a likely outcome while also acknowledging that we have the power to shift this at any time, as no future is set in stone.

Write journal entries as you read your spread. The following are some journal prompts to consider:

→ What outcome would satisfy me the most?

→ Which past events are weighing the heaviest on me currently?

→ In what ways, if any, am I allowing the influence of others to affect me?

→ In what ways does my fear keep me from reaching a favorable outcome?

→ How can I begin to release the past so I may align with my hopes?

→ What did I learn from this spread that I didn't already know?

DESIGNING YOUR OWN SPREADS

One of the most enjoyable aspects of reading tarot is designing your own spreads! The key to designing an effective spread is having a clear intention and purpose for your reading. There are unlimited combinations of questions and scenarios you can make up.

The basic formula begins with any subject to represent the overall energy of your spread. Think about what the spread will *do*. Do you want to design a spread that reveals unknowns, offers guidance, or makes connections? Then consider who and what it will explore. Will it relate to present events, will it focus exclusively on matters of the heart, or will it illuminate issues that exist between two people?

Next, get curious. What do you want to know about your subject? What are your intuitive feelings about the subject? Follow up by asking for messages and advice from your higher self or divine guidance on what to do with your subject, and build from there. Remember to create spreads that answer productive questions that encourage action, and avoid providing concrete answers about when or how something will happen. (Instead of "When will I get a raise?" try "How should I focus my energy to increase my income?")

Basic Formula

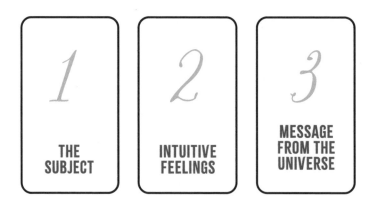

1	*2*	*3*
THE SUBJECT	INTUITIVE FEELINGS	MESSAGE FROM THE UNIVERSE

CHAPTER 4

Major Arcana

· ·

THE MAJOR ARCANA is a subset
within the tarot deck that consists of 22
trump cards, or cards that rank above the
others. They present the pictorial story
of the Fool's journey, beginning with the
Fool (0) himself and ending with the
World (21). The Major Arcana represents
big life events and important lessons—
both individual and collective—that
shape our lives. In this chapter, you'll find
the basic numerological, planetary, and
astrological signs that correspond to each
card, along with the universal meanings
that apply to almost every tarot deck.

· ·

0 ✳ THE FOOL

The Fool embarks on a new journey, leaving the past behind, carrying with him only the lessons learned and a curiosity to begin again.

....

Each card carries the energy of the ones that come before it, beginning with the Fool, who carries the energy of the zero (0), a symbol that contains everything and nothing at the same time. The Fool progresses through the lessons and events shown by each card of the Major Arcana, growing, experiencing, and maturing as his consciousness evolves. In the imagery on the Fool's card, you see a young person in a floral print tunic. The Fool looks to the bright yellow sky, with the sun to his back and blissfully unaware that he is about to walk off a cliff. Carrying only a bindle and a white rose, he is innocent and free of life's burdens. He's ready to take on whatever may come his way, with arms outstretched, suggesting openness to new possibilities without fear of failure. A small dog prances alongside the Fool, attempting to alert him of the dangerous cliff he is headed toward. This is the path of unfolding consciousness, a symbol of the Fool's willingness to meet life's challenges in order to make progress.

UPRIGHT KEY MEANINGS

New beginning, freedom

REVERSED KEY MEANINGS

Naiveté, fear of change

NUMEROLOGY

0, an open container, encompassing everything and nothing

ASTROLOGY

Uranus (sudden change, freedom)

GENERAL READING

This is where your adventure begins! The Fool knows he is on the right path, even if he does not know where it will lead. Be willing to take a risk, with the knowledge that every big leap forward may have its pitfalls and that setbacks are lessons that will guide you on your journey. Your intuition is always by your side, much like the little dog who walks with the Fool. Tune into its guidance and heed its messages as your own path to expanded consciousness unfolds.

LOVE/ROMANCE

Drawing the Fool in a reading about romance indicates the querent should take a chance on love or be open to a new beginning within an existing relationship. Trust intuition, and leave the past behind. It's never too late to begin again.

CAREER/MONEY

Take a risk and try something new. Everything may not run smoothly, but being bold is the only way to get to the next level in your career. Listen to your own inner guidance and you may experience beginner's luck.

PERSONAL/SPIRITUAL

Take a leap of faith and trust that you have the support of the universe. Don't be afraid of the unknown. Instead, acknowledge that the lessons you encounter will lead to expanded consciousness and unforeseen opportunities. They are a part of your personal and spiritual evolution.

REVERSED

A reversed Fool in your readings can signal that it's not the right time to take a risk or jump into something. It may mean that you're being challenged by your fear of change or experiencing hesitation to step out of your comfort zone. There is a naiveté with this card, so it may mean to move forward later on, once you have a solid plan.

REFLECT ....

→ Where in your life are you engaging with the energy of the Fool?

1 ✳ THE MAGICIAN

The Magician has the power of the four elements: earth, air, fire, and water, combined with their connection to the divine. They are able to create unlimited abundance in the physical realm.

Now that the Fool has taken the leap into the unknown, he meets the Magician and learns that the power of the universe is within him to create his own reality! A robed figure stands with a wand in one hand, pointed toward the sky, and the other hand pointed at the ground. The infinity symbol and body posture represent the Magician's connection between the spiritual and physical realms. On the table are items representing the four elemental suits: a wand (fire), a pentacle (earth), a sword (air), and a cup (water). These were the contents of the Fool's bindle! By drawing upon the powers of the elements and the help of the divine, the Magician serves as a conduit, with the power to give form to the formless by transforming intentions into actions to achieve physical results. The flowers and vegetation symbolize his connection to nature and signify that purity (white) and passion (red) are both essential to the creation process. With divine assistance, all things are possible.

UPRIGHT KEY MEANINGS
Manifestation, creator, inspired action

REVERSED KEY MEANINGS
Disconnection from personal power, manipulative

NUMEROLOGY
1, the beginning, the individual

ASTROLOGY
Mercury (messages, communication)

GENERAL READING

You are the Magician, and the elemental ingredients you need to be creative are always at your fingertips! With clear intention and passion, you can connect to the divine and manifest your dreams into reality. This card is a reminder that you are more powerful than you know. Take action when inspired, and focus on keeping each element in balance in your life. When you take action on your dreams and desires, you create your world.

LOVE/ROMANCE

Drawing the Magician in a reading about romance can mean manifesting a wonderful relationship or reigniting the spark within an existing one. You have everything within you to create the relationship of your dreams, regardless of your relationship status. Pay attention to balancing your emotions (water) with your thoughts (air) while remaining grounded (earth) and passionate (fire).

CAREER/MONEY

You can create new opportunities, using all of your inherent skills to cultivate abundance, manifest prosperity, and take inspired action toward goals. If you've been wanting to start your own business, now is the time. Know your worth when negotiating for a raise or contract.

PERSONAL/SPIRITUAL

You are coming into your power by working with nature and spirit. Drawing this card signifies deepening your spiritual practice and co-creating your reality with the universe/divine.

REVERSED

The reversed Magician can point to misuse of power, manipulation, or trying to force a situation. You may be doubting your ability to create and manifest or experiencing a possible block to your connection with an important aspect of your identity. This is a time to reconnect to the source of power within you. Trust that if the door isn't opening, there may be a better door elsewhere . . . or another way in. If you feel blocked, redirect your energies.

REFLECT ···

→ How are you acting as the Magician in your life?

2 ✳ THE HIGH PRIESTESS

The High Priestess, like the moon, sees through the darkness, illuminating what is hidden, reminding us that all we need to know is already within us.

Seated between two columns, one light and one dark, the High Priestess represents the balance that exists naturally in our dual natures. Her headdress evokes the waxing, full, and waning phases of the moon, symbolizing the progression of seasons of a woman's life from maiden to mother to wise crone. The religious icons she wears and holds include the cross and the Torah, which reflect the popular beliefs of the time period during which the deck was created but are also symbolic of the High Priestess's devotion to her spiritual practice. Behind her hangs a tapestry covered with pomegranates—symbols of fertility and feminine energy—that obstruct her view of the water, representing emotions. The crescent moon at her feet symbolizes her connection to lunar power and intuition. Although the High Priestess has her back to the water, she does not need to see it with her eyes; she is connected to her emotions from within.

UPRIGHT KEY MEANINGS

Intuition, self-knowledge

REVERSED KEY MEANINGS

Disconnection from intuition, refusal to look within

NUMEROLOGY

2, duality, balance, harmony

ASTROLOGY

The moon (emotions, intuition, feminine energy)

GENERAL READING

Connecting to the divine is an internal process. Your intuitive, higher self can be channeled at any time by looking within. The High Priestess urges you to clear your mind and ask your heart for the answers you seek. The answers are already within you!

LOVE/RELATIONSHIP

Listen to your intuition. Emotional intelligence will lead you to the answers you need about your romantic urges. What does your gut say about your relationship? Trust your feelings instead of overthinking or overanalyzing.

CAREER/MONEY

Follow intuitive urges when making financial and business decisions, even if you're tempted to investigate endlessly. Know that you have the answers rather than relying on other people's opinions. Make intuitive choices in business rather than over-intellectualizing or rationalizing.

PERSONAL/SPIRITUAL

Go within to connect to your divine guidance, since strengthening your intuition deepens your spiritual practice. Trust yourself and follow your intuition, even if where it leads you might not make logical sense at first.

REVERSED

The reversed High Priestess often signifies a disconnection from your intuition. You may be looking for answers outside of yourself, relying too heavily on the guidance of others, or allowing yourself to be influenced. This is a reminder to tap back into the source within for answers, even if that feels uncomfortable at first.

REFLECT ··

→ What connections does the High Priestess want you to make within yourself?

3 ✳ THE EMPRESS

The Empress embodies the essence of divine feminine energy. Through her connection to nature and her willingness to let her body be a sacred vessel, she creates a life filled with love.

The Empress sits on plush pillows in a lush forest while a river flows toward her, suggesting her connection to nature. A heart with the symbol of Venus is proudly displayed by her side, indicating she is open to love and beauty in all their forms. Her flowing pomegranate-print gown symbolizes passion, fertility, and the ability to create. On her head is a crown of stars representing the 12 signs of the zodiac. The Empress's raised scepter and open body posture reveal her receptiveness and her confident attitude about the power of her sexuality.

UPRIGHT KEY MEANINGS
Receiving love, creativity

REVERSED KEY MEANING
Disconnection, creative blocks

NUMEROLOGY
3, creativity, growth, expansion

ASTROLOGY
Venus (love, beauty, money, creativity)

GENERAL READING

The Empress emanates a powerful energy of receiving rather than taking action. You can allow what is being birthed in your life to take its time without rushing or forcing it. The Empress is relaxed, trusting that her passion and creativity produces a powerful magnetism that attracts everything she desires.

LOVE/ROMANCE

Allow yourself to receive love, and acknowledge that you can attract romance by loving yourself. This is a fertile time for you that may lead to a pregnancy. You are drawing love to yourself naturally and in your own time.

CAREER/MONEY

You may be receiving money or a job from unexpected sources, creating even more abundance in your life. But since this card is about receptivity, be careful not to push. You will need to be patient.

PERSONAL/SPIRITUAL

Remember to practice self-love and engage in more creative activities. By tapping into the energy of Venus through creativity, romance, self-love, and spending time in nature, you can bring divine love into your spiritual practice. Go outside and find ways to connect with the natural world.

REVERSED

The reversed Empress can point to the ways you feel blocked or cut off from loving yourself or allowing others to love and care for you. You may be feeling disconnected from your creativity or unable to receive praise, affection, or other signals of positivity. The reversed Empress may also suggest difficulties in pregnancy, romantic complications, or trying to force a situation rather than being patient. It can indicate that you're relying too heavily on masculine energy to make things happen, and a need to tap into feminine energy instead. Consider finding ways to reconnect with nature to remind yourself that everything blooms in its own time.

REFLECT

→ What are you creating in your world with your Empress energy?

4 ✳ THE EMPEROR

The Emperor sits on his heavy throne, clad in armor beneath his robes. He is grounded yet ready for action at all times.

....

The Emperor embodies the divine masculine counterpart and action-oriented energy. He sits on a concrete throne adorned with rams, symbolizing his stability and connection to the astrological sign of Aries. The landscape behind him is barren, except for a stream of water flowing through the scene, representing emotion and intuition, which lead him to take inspired action when necessary. He wears a crown and holds an orb and scepter representing his authority and power, and beneath his robe is armor that suggests he is ready to jump into battle at any moment. Notice the colors in this card. Reds and oranges are symbolic of power, authority, and assertiveness in the material realm.

UPRIGHT KEY MEANINGS

Inspired action, personal power

REVERSED KEY MEANINGS

Inability to take action, or defensive/reactive

NUMEROLOGY

4, stability, structure

ASTROLOGY

Aries (individuality, personal power)

GENERAL READING

The connection to divine masculine energy in the Emperor card is what leads you to take action from a place of power rather than reacting from a place of fear. This requires having a healthy relationship to your masculine energy and taking up space. Connect to your inner authority, acknowledging ambition, drive, and power in a way that serves the greater good, not just yourself.

LOVE/ROMANCE

Make a move, be bold, and heed your passions. You have more power in the realm of romance than you realize. Stay balanced with the masculine energy by noting when you're being too assertive or not assertive enough in your relationships. Your intuition will guide you to where more or less of this energy is needed.

CAREER/MONEY

If you've been waiting for a sign to take inspired action on your goals, this is it. It's time to speak up or step fully into a leadership role. Being more aggressive in issues related to your career will work in your favor, so go ahead and ask for what you want.

PERSONAL/SPIRITUAL

To tap into that active, masculine energy, try utilizing affirmations of self-empowerment. Give yourself permission to take up more space and become the authority within your life (instead of deferring to others or valuing their opinions over your own).

REVERSED

The reversed Emperor in a reading can suggest a disconnection from personal power or an inability to take action. Let that bold, assertive masculine energy flow so you can stand up for yourself or take control of a situation. This reversal can also indicate the presence of toxic masculine energy, the abuse of power, defensiveness, or immature reactions that stem from fear and anger.

REFLECT

→ How do you identify with the Emperor?

5 ✳ THE HIEROPHANT

The Hierophant sits upon a temple throne, sharing his sacred knowledge with devoted pupils. Through his connection to spirit, he is the bridge between heaven and earth.

· ·

A "hierophant" is an interpreter of sacred mysteries or esoteric principles, so this card evokes an ongoing quest for knowledge. Much like the High Priestess, the Hierophant is in near-constant communication with the divine. The difference is that the High Priestess channels her knowledge through her intuition, while the Hierophant studies and learns by upholding traditions, participating in rituals, and teaching ancient knowledge to others. The Hierophant appears seated on a throne in traditional religious robes, busily sharing his spiritual teachings with the two figures seated before him. The religious iconography—the keys and his papal staff, hand position, and crosses, to name a few—is symbolic of his purity and devotion to his spirituality. Having strong faith and a set of strict principles to live by, the Hierophant is happiest following a traditional course of study.

UPRIGHT KEY MEANINGS
Teacher, tradition

REVERSED KEY MEANINGS
Rigid beliefs, refusal to learn

NUMEROLOGY
5, conflict, struggle, challenges

ASTROLOGY
Taurus (traditional, grounded, rigid)

GENERAL READING

The path of learning is never complete. Remain open to new courses of study, and honor tradition while also forming your own unique set of beliefs and rituals. When you are ready to learn, be alert to the presence of a potential new teacher in your life. On the other hand, this teacher could be you, if you are in a position to share your wisdom with others.

LOVE/ROMANCE

When it comes to the institution of marriage, you may have strong beliefs about romance and partnerships. Drawing this card may also mean that you are dedicated to taking a traditional path in love. Occasionally, the Hierophant signals a romantic relationship with someone you consider a teacher or student, or perhaps a budding relationship in which you learn from one another constantly.

CAREER/MONEY

This card indicates a traditional career path or move up the ladder of success. It may also nudge you toward earning

money as a teacher, going back to school, or studying a new subject to further your current career.

PERSONAL/SPIRITUAL

You may deepen your spirituality by studying healing modalities or courses in the foundations of spiritual knowledge. You may even teach healing arts or offer spiritual guidance. Be open to a teacher entering your life; this may come in many forms.

REVERSED

The reversed Hierophant in a reading often signifies a detour or roadblock in the querent's spiritual path or course of study. It indicates rigid beliefs, a refusal to remain open to alternative information, or a resistance to learning new things. If this reversal appears in your reading, take it as a reminder to try to have an open mind and be respectful of opposing viewpoints.

REFLECT

→ The Hierophant asks: what are you ready to learn?

6 ✳ THE LOVERS

The Lovers stand together in harmony, the balance of masculine and feminine, with nothing to hide. Every choice they make is in alignment with love.

The Lovers card signifies an opportunity to connect in relationships that support your happiest, healthiest, best self. The imagery shows a man and a woman standing naked in a garden between the tree of life and the tree of knowledge. The snake represents the temptation to indulge in earthly pleasures, while the angel encourages the couple to choose divine love over succumbing to instant gratification. Desire for pleasure is balanced by vulnerability and trust, since both exist within a harmonious relationship.

UPRIGHT KEY MEANINGS
Relationship, alignment

REVERSED KEY MEANING
Disharmony, imbalance

NUMEROLOGY
6, harmony, reciprocity, mirror image

ASTROLOGY
Gemini (duality, communication, adaptability)

GENERAL READING

You always have the choice to align with divine love by balancing masculine and feminine energy within yourself, and you can strive to ensure that this balance is reflected in your relationships. Choosing relationships with mutual respect and healthy communication will lead you to the highest expression of love you seek.

LOVE/RELATIONSHIPS

Romantic connection is available, or an opportunity for love is near or already in front of you. Use your values to guide your relationship choices. This card may signify an important relationship or soul mate in your life, or one that is about to enter your life.

CAREER/MONEY

There may be romance in the workplace, or you may be working with your romantic partner. It may also mean aligning with a beneficial business partner or coworker. You could also be making money in alignment with what you love.

PERSONAL/SPIRITUAL

This card serves as a reminder to choose divine love over instant gratification and that balancing masculine and feminine energies within yourself will attract the right relationships to you.

REVERSED

The reversed Lovers in your reading can point to a relationship that is out of balance, or codependent. This can also point to relying too heavily on a partner to fulfill your needs, or having unrealistic expectations of your relationships. To fix the imbalance, look inward to see where you can find the source of disharmony. Happiness is an inside job that is reflected in our relationships.

REFLECT

→ If the Lovers were having a conversation, what would they be saying to one another?

7 ✳ THE CHARIOT

Guided by our intuition, the Chariot is the structure that protects us while we are taking inspired action.

....

A symbol of building momentum, the Chariot card signals that you are beginning to create your plan of action. This card shows a man in armor at the reins and ready for battle, yet the Chariot itself is not in motion. This is because the Chariot represents the solid foundation of forethought that is needed before one can jump into action. The pair of sphinxes at the front of the Chariot are lying motionless on the ground, and their only sign of movement is their eyes gazing in opposing directions. They appear to be surveying their surroundings, considering which way to go. The river behind the scene, a symbol of emotions, suggests the importance of awaiting intuitive guidance before taking any action. A canopy of stars above the charioteer's head represents the value of looking to the cosmos for guidance, while his armor signifies his connection to the zodiac sign Cancer's hard outer shell of protection.

UPRIGHT KEY MEANINGS
Inspired action, momentum

REVERSED KEY MEANINGS
Inability to move
forward, stagnation

NUMEROLOGY
7, personal growth,
planning, assessing

ASTROLOGY
Cancer (nurturing, protective,
intuitive)

GENERAL READING

You are embarking on an important journey or moving toward the next level of your life goals! The Chariot asks you to have a clear intention, focus, and a plan for action. Sheer determination alone isn't enough to propel you toward success. Building a solid foundation and creating structure are both necessary steps before you can make big decisions. If you're not sure what to tackle right now, listen to your intuition to guide you toward the next actionable steps.

LOVE/ROMANCE

You are moving fast in a relationship, but do you both have the same vision for the future? Create a solid foundation and establish any plans before taking this relationship to the next level.

CAREER/MONEY

Now is the time to create a clear, concise business plan while also taking intuitively inspired action toward your career or financial goals. Success comes with focus, determination, and clear intention.

PERSONAL/SPIRITUAL

You're ready to take your spiritual practice to the next level, which means you're gaining momentum in life. Based on your intention of moving forward, you can utilize your spiritual practice to guide you to the next phases of life with confidence.

REVERSED

The reversed Chariot in a reading can suggest a lack of confidence around a specific goal or a general lack of focus or direction. It signals the need for a more concrete plan in order to regain momentum. Impulse control will be needed in order to grow and take action in a positive direction. This reversal may also warn of moving too quickly, missing important steps, or hesitation.

REFLECT

→ Where do you think the Chariot is going?

VIII

STRENGTH.

8 ✳ STRENGTH

Strength reminds us that it is not the size of our muscles, but the willingness within our hearts, that matters. When we show courage, we can endure any obstacles we encounter.

The Strength card shows a woman wearing a white robe adorned with flowers—suggesting her purity of heart—demonstrating her own strength by gently closing the mouth of a lion. The woman represents receptive, feminine energy but not weakness. Without fear or hesitation, she courageously lays her hands on a wild and ferocious beast. The lion's pliant and submissive body language indicates that it does not feel threatened by her touch. The infinity symbol above her head is a reminder that the energy within us always manifests in our outer circumstances. This woman is peaceful within, and that peacefulness is reflected in her dealings in the world. Approaching an obstacle with confidence and acting in a calm way will yield positive results for all involved.

UPRIGHT KEY MEANINGS
Overcoming obstacles, endurance

REVERSED KEY MEANINGS
Apprehension, lacking confidence

NUMEROLOGY
8, progress, decisive action

ASTROLOGY
Leo (courageous, heart-centered)

GENERAL READING

You are stronger than you know! Life is full of challenges, but you can trust yourself to handle just about any situation that arises. Let the infinity symbol remind you that you are capable of overcoming struggles both internally and externally. Strength asks you to be present with your fears rather than pushing them down and move forward with courage even when your confidence wavers.

LOVE/ROMANCE

Have confidence and put yourself out there to meet new people. Do not be afraid to show your vulnerability and share your heart with your partner if you are actively overcoming obstacles in your relationship.

CAREER/MONEY

Have confidence and persistence in your career—there is power in your voice. You can effectively reach the next level financially by taking a firm, subtle approach. You can move past any hurdles and achieve a successful outcome in your work, so don't give up or doubt your strength.

PERSONAL/SPIRITUAL

Whether you're making changes in your life or working to reach the next deepest level of your connection with the divine, you have what it takes within you to overcome any challenges. Be brave and trust your inner strength, but know it's perfectly fine to be vulnerable. Feel your fears and take action anyway!

REVERSED

The reversed Strength card in a reading can suggest a lack of self-confidence, wavering trust in yourself, or a reluctance to have faith in the universe. It can also point to feeling apprehensive about taking action, feeling weak, or being uncomfortable with vulnerability.

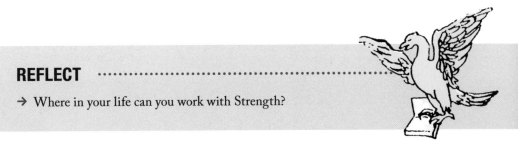

REFLECT

→ Where in your life can you work with Strength?

9 ✶ THE HERMIT

The Hermit is wise, and he knows the difference between being alone and being lonely; his solitude is the companion to his bright mind.

There is wisdom to be gained through solitude; this is the lesson that the Hermit card imparts. On it, an old man walks alone, carrying a tall staff and a lantern to light his way. The lantern illuminates only on what's in front of him, but points him toward the truth. His advanced age signals deep wisdom, while the staff suggests power. His power is in his ability to look within, rely on himself, and exercise tremendous patience.

UPRIGHT KEY MEANINGS
Wisdom, solitude

REVERSE KEY MEANINGS
Loneliness, isolation

NUMEROLOGY
9, nearing completion, solitude

ASTROLOGY
Virgo (analytical, hard-working, patient)

GENERAL READING

Many people fear being alone, but spending time by yourself to explore your inner worlds empowers you to connect deeply to your inner truth. Listening to your inner wisdom by spending time in solitude is a necessary and healthy practice that will rejuvenate you. When it's time to be with others again, you will feel your energy restored.

LOVE/ROMANCE

Time alone is best right now. You need some space for yourself to connect with your personal truths. Consider taking a break from love and romance for some soul-searching. Spending some time apart from a partner can enable you to come back together stronger than before.

CAREER/MONEY

Take some space to connect to your own natural intelligence and inclinations, and feel free to block out the opinions of others. If you're considering applying for a promotion, making an investment, or exploring a new idea, you don't need anyone else's permission to move ahead. Working alone, rather than in collaboration, is best at this time.

PERSONAL/SPIRITUAL

You're deep in the process of soul-searching and seeking your own inner truth. Allow yourself as much time alone as you need to look within, perhaps through meditation or taking long walks to tap into your divine inner wisdom.

REVERSED

The reversed Hermit in a reading can indicate a fear of being alone, or refusal to look within yourself. It may also mean you've been in isolation for too long, and it's time to reach out for support and connection. Use your intuition to guide you toward the meaning that resonates.

REFLECT ....

→ What wisdom does the Hermit have to share with you?

WHEEL of FORTUNE.

10 ✴ WHEEL OF FORTUNE

The Wheel of Fortune is always turning, illustrating that each moment is temporary and that life is cyclical, not linear. Surrender to the present.

The Wheel of Fortune card allows you to gain a deeper understanding of life's cycles of change. Its imagery has mystical, astrological, and occult symbolism, showing that many of the forces influencing our lives are mysterious and invisible. The wheel appears to float through the clouds, indicating that our spiritual path is connected to the physical realm. The creatures in the clouds are zodiac signs: Aquarius (air), Scorpio (water), Taurus (earth), and Leo (fire). They represent the stable forces that uphold the wheel itself. Beneath the wheel is Anubis, the Egyptian god of the dead, who represents life, death, and rebirth. The sphinx sits atop the wheel, a multifaceted creature representing the diversity of life. The downward-facing snake is symbolic of life's challenges everyone must face. All of the creatures and symbols rotate around the wheel, teaching us that life has its ups and downs in an ever-changing cycle. We all must embrace the temporary nature of each moment. Change is the only true constant.

UPRIGHT KEY MEANINGS
Cycles, change

REVERSED KEY MEANINGS
Delays, setbacks

NUMEROLOGY
10, completion of a cycle

ASTROLOGY
Jupiter (luck, expansion, growth)

GENERAL READING

Cultivating a strong spiritual practice can ease negative moments, help us enjoy the positive moments, and empower us to navigate the uncertain and challenging moments in our lives. By understanding the cycles of life on a deeper level, we build our own strength and resilience. The Wheel of Fortune asks you to focus on what you can control in order to find peace within the uncertainty of change and to let go of anything you cannot control. By doing this, you open yourself up to fated events and meetings without forcing your fate. What is meant for you will not miss you!

LOVE/ROMANCE

This card signals a chance or fated meeting with a new romantic partner, though it can also symbolize completion of a cycle in your love life. Alternatively, you may be entering a new phase of a relationship that has existed for some time already. The Wheel of Fortune shows your luck may be changing in romance and the possibility of wonderful new experiences after a time of sadness.

CAREER/MONEY

New beginnings or fated events are unfolding to move you along the path of good fortune, job opportunities, and unexpected wealth. One career or financial cycle is coming to a close and transitioning into the next. Stay the course; your luck is shifting.

PERSONAL/SPIRITUAL

Fate is currently leading you forward on your path. You are moving from a painful cycle to a more harmonious one with new understanding and faith. You trust in the process of life, the cycles of death and rebirth, meeting new people, and embracing new situations that have entered your life.

REVERSED

The reversed Wheel of Fortune in your reading asks you to focus on what you can control when things feel chaotic. Are you refusing to let something come to an end or resisting growth? Everything is changing around you, which can feel uncomfortable, but this time of instability is temporary. What is ending now will create space for something new to come in its place.

REFLECT

→ What single question would you ask the Wheel of Fortune?

11 ✳ JUSTICE

Justice is served by restoring divine balance through upholding and committing to the truth.

The message of this card is: that which has been unstable is rebalanced. Justice is seated between two pillars, a figure holding the sword of truth in one hand and the scales of justice in the other. The figure appears to be a judge who is committed to remaining objective in her quest for veracity. Her red robe symbolizes being grounded in the material world, while the yellow crown and background peeking out from behind the curtain symbolize her state of harmony with the spiritual elements that exist within the physical realm. The presence of the sword suggests she prefers using logic over emotions, a sentiment echoed by the crown on her head, emphasizing the power of the mind.

UPRIGHT KEY MEANINGS
Truth, balance

REVERSED KEY MEANINGS
Imbalance, unfair treatment

NUMEROLOGY
1 + 1 = 2. Connected to The High Priestess (2).

ASTROLOGY
Libra (balance, truth, partnership)

GENERAL READING

Justice asks you to use logic and remain objective, as this will help you uncover the truth within each situation. She indicates that positive outcomes in legal matters or unsettled interpersonal issues are inevitable; all you need to do is stay true to yourself and act with integrity. Have faith that imbalanced situations are now working out in your favor.

LOVE/ROMANCE

Disputes and disagreements are moving inevitably toward resolution. You can look forward to restoring balance within a relationship, standing up for your needs, or being willing to hear the other person's side and reach a mutually beneficial compromise. After a period of discord, you are now able to come to an agreement.

CAREER/MONEY

Fair agreements are being made and disputes resolved. You're finding balance in the workplace, speaking your truth in a business situation, working toward positive outcomes in a legal matter, or maybe even signing contracts that will move your career forward.

PERSONAL/SPIRITUAL

The Justice card signifies reconciling the past; finding balance, alignment, and harmony within; and fulfilling karmic contracts. In a reading about your inner life, it points toward restoring balance within the spiritual world.

REVERSED

The reversed Justice card in your reading can indicate a struggle to achieve balance. Perhaps something unfair has recently transpired, or an event that was not aligned with your personal ethics needs your attention. Your intuition will guide you to what that represents in your life. Once you've identified where that is you can begin to look into how to shift the energy surrounding the situation if possible. Sometimes, no matter how hard you try, difficulties still arise.

REFLECT ••

→ In which aspects of your life are you seeking Justice?

12 ✳ THE HANGED MAN

When you are suspended upside down, there is time to reflect and see things from a new perspective.

....

The Hanged Man offers the unusual gift of suspended time. His presence is associated with a time period that is meant to help shift your perception of a situation. The Hanged Man is suspended by one leg, upside down, from the tree of life. His hands appear to be tied behind his back. His free leg is crossed behind the bound leg and appears relaxed and resting. He has nowhere to go, so he is able to sit quietly in reflection, which shows on his face. He is calm, almost pensive, rather than distressed. Yellow illumination surrounds his head, suggesting spiritual enlightenment is occurring during this time of pause. This is a time to surrender, not struggle.

UPRIGHT KEY MEANINGS
Waiting, shifting perspective

REVERSED KEY MEANINGS
Impatience, inertia

NUMEROLOGY
1 + 2 = 3. Connected to The Empress (3).

ASTROLOGY
Neptune (dreams, illusions)

GENERAL READING

During moments when no forward movement can be made, you have the opportunity to see your situation from a new perspective. Getting curious about what you can learn from this forced waiting period will lead to new spiritual insights. Surrender to what is happening, and find peace during moments of inactivity until the time is right for action and transformation.

LOVE/ROMANCE

The current situation isn't moving forward for a reason, so take a moment to engage with this feeling of limbo. It is here to teach you something. Now is not the time to move forward, which means you can work on seeing your situation from another perspective. Trust that the timing is perfect, even if it feels uncomfortable.

CAREER/MONEY

Waiting will yield better results, so take this waiting period to expand your vision by seeing your situation from multiple viewpoints. Do not make any hasty decisions right now concerning your finances or career path. Wait until a clearer signal for action emerges.

PERSONAL/SPIRITUAL

Unexpected moments of pause can lead to new spiritual insights. Gaining a new perspective on your situation helps you expand your beliefs. Take time to reflect and surrender to the present moment as fully as you can.

REVERSED

The reversed Hanged Man in your reading is telling you not to fight your current circumstances or force forward movement. Delays are annoying, but the divine is trying to show you something you may have otherwise missed before. You may feel eager to begin the next part of your journey, but instead quiet your mind and listen for intuitive messages. There is much to be gained in stillness.

REFLECT ···

→ What new perspective might the Hanged Man have to offer on a difficult situation in your life?

13 ✳ DEATH

*Death is the ultimate transformation,
a cycle of release leading to rebirth.*

Death is perhaps one of the most misunderstood cards in the tarot, and one that is overflowing with rich symbolism. Death appears as a skeleton dressed in black armor riding through a scene of figures near death or already dead, holding a black flag with a flower and ears of corn on it, representing the growing and harvesting seasons that align with the seasons of our lives. A religious figure appears to plead with Death, while a child and a young woman kneel nearby, both symbolizing innocence in transition. In the distance, the sun rises between two towers, representing the conscious and unconscious mind. The skeleton is yellow, the color of spiritual enlightenment, as are the robes of the religious figure. The horse he rides symbolizes the freedom that arises from embracing transformation, and the fact that he is seated on his horse looking down at the religious figure suggests that spiritual enlightenment transcends traditional religious teachings. The sun rising illuminates rebirth, a contrast to Death's black armor, which indicates that shadow aspects once hidden are now displayed with pride. Death is protected during this cycle of change, as are we all during times of transformation.

UPRIGHT KEY MEANINGS

Transformation, release

REVERSED KEY MEANINGS

Clinging to the past,
refusing to change

NUMEROLOGY

1 + 3 = 4. Connected
to The Emperor (4).

ASTROLOGY

Scorpio (transformation,
power, protection)

GENERAL READING

Remember that life is a continuous cycle of death and rebirth, and that change is natural. Seasons shift, and you yourself shift and grow as you evolve along your personal path. Death asks you to surrender to this cycle and release the things in your life that have outlived their purposes. This isn't an easy process, but take comfort in knowing that something more suited for the next phase of your life is coming to replace what has left.

LOVE/ROMANCE

This card signals the transformation of a relationship, possibly in a radical or unexpected way. While it may be painful to let go of certain aspects, doing so creates space for something new and beautiful to thrive. The end is also the beginning.

CAREER/MONEY

Ending one phase of your career may be accompanied by some grief, but this is part of the cycle of renewal and transformation that brings you to the next phase. The Death card says in no uncertain terms that it is time to move on.

PERSONAL/SPIRITUAL

You're in the throes of a transformation of the self that may include letting go of old, worn-out patterns and behaviors. This purge is creating space for new beginnings by forcing you to release the past.

REVERSED

The reversed Death card in your reading can suggest that you are clinging to something in your life that is ready to be released. You are resisting moving forward or stubbornly hanging on to the past. This card tells you that surrendering to change can be scary, but also that resistance can prolong the cycle and amplify the pain. Let go, and trust in the universe and yourself.

REFLECT ···

→ What single question would you ask Death about the transformation you are undergoing?

14 TEMPERANCE

Temperance teaches us to call on the angelic realm for support in taking a balanced approach, yielding results that are better than we could obtain on our own.

....

Temperance reveals a promising path forward, but one that requires us to reach out for assistance from the divine. An angel stands with one foot on land and one foot in the water as they pour water back and forth between cups. The water appears to flow in both directions at once, representing the process of alchemy wherein the impossible becomes possible through a connection with the divine. This card tells you that if you choose a path of thoughtful moderation, the divine will support you by taking action on your behalf. This is how alchemy works in the spiritual realm.

UPRIGHT KEY MEANINGS

Moderation, harmony, divine timing

REVERSED KEY MEANINGS

Imbalance, pushing for results

NUMEROLOGY

1 + 4 = 5. Connected to The Hierophant (5).

ASTROLOGY

Sagittarius (adventure, seeking higher wisdom and truth, optimism)

GENERAL READING

When you are working toward achieving something in your life, you don't have to do it alone! Call upon divine assistance for help, look for signs, and follow inspired guidance when those signs appear before you. Be flexible and take a moderate approach, trusting that the results you want will take time. Have patience as the universe goes to work to bring your desires into the physical realm.

LOVE/ROMANCE

Do not force a relationship right now. The universe is working behind the scenes to bring romance into your life, so trust that divine timing. Seek balance and harmony in existing relationships, and ask the universe for divine guidance to achieve what you desire.

CAREER/MONEY

Timing is a factor in your work and financial life right now, so ask for messages and divine assistance to create abundance and career opportunities. Be patient and have faith. When you trust that events will take their course, abundance will unfold before you.

PERSONAL/SPIRITUAL

Whether you are struggling with something specific or just feeling lost, now is the perfect time to connect with the divine and welcome the messages you receive. Use your intuitive guidance to move forward on your path to reach your highest self. Surrender to the plans of the universe.

REVERSED

The reversed Temperance card in your reading can indicate you are trying too hard or forcing a situation instead of relaxing and allowing it to unfold in divine timing. It can also indicate that some form of moderation is needed in order to reestablish alignment with your highest path. The divine is counseling you to find balance and avoid extreme situations and behaviors.

REFLECT ·······································

→ What can Temperance teach you about balance and trusting in divine timing?

THE DEVIL .

15 ✳ THE DEVIL

The Devil shows us the places in our lives where we are chained to self-sabotage. Through this understanding, we set ourselves free.

The Devil is another card that is often misunderstood and widely believed to be an ill omen. In truth, there is nothing to fear from the Devil once his meaning is illuminated. The card depicts a literal devil that is partly human in appearance, but with horns, wings, and a beastly looking lower half, symbolic of the things we demonize or fear. A reversed pentagram crowns him, representing his connection to dark energy. Beneath the Devil stand a man and a woman in chains, who look almost identical to the Lovers. Their state of being chained to the Devil represents our addictions, self-sabotaging behaviors, unhealthy coping mechanisms, and fears. When we cultivate awareness and take responsibility for our actions, only then can we liberate ourselves from these chains. The Devil card shows us where our internal misalignments lie.

UPRIGHT KEY MEANINGS
Sabotage, addiction

REVERSED KEY MEANINGS
Release, liberation

NUMEROLOGY
1 + 5 = 6. Connected to The Lovers (6). They are two sides of the same coin—one light, one dark.

ASTROLOGY
Capricorn (ambitious, pessimistic, responsible)

GENERAL READING

The Devil comes as a gentle confrontation about self-destructive thoughts or behaviors. Using your intuition, ask yourself what unhealthy habits or coping mechanisms are present in your life. Identifying the fears that lead to self-sabotaging behavior doesn't have to be a scary process. Instead, it can be illuminating, much like the Devil's torch that lights the darkness of the card.

LOVE/ROMANCE

This card warns of the presence of an unhealthy or toxic relationship, perhaps one that involves choosing lust over love, codependency, or a controlling partner. However, it may also be telling you that experimentation with power and control in the bedroom can spice up a healthy relationship.

CAREER/MONEY

You are nurturing an unhealthy relationship to money or indulging workaholic tendencies. The Devil can indicate that you are due to release yourself from a situation involving a controlling boss or toxic work environment. Perhaps you are staying in a job for the wrong reasons.

PERSONAL/SPIRITUAL

It may be time to examine toxic thought patterns and unhealthy coping mechanisms so you can get to the root cause of ongoing self-sabotage in order to free yourself. If what you are doing feels good in the moment, does it have negative aftereffects?

REVERSED

The reversed Devil in a reading can be a good sign, pointing to a renewal of hope or abandonment of a toxic or unhealthy situation. This card in reverse points to freedom from an old and destructive pattern. It also can suggest that making a difficult or unpopular decision will be for the best.

REFLECT ···

→ What unhealthy attachments does the Devil want you to recognize?

16 * THE TOWER

The Tower reminds us that what is breaking down is allowing something else to break free.

The Tower is the third most misunderstood card in the tarot, with imagery that depicts destruction, loss of stability, and violent lack of control. When sudden change sweeps your comfort zone out from underneath you, it's scary and upsetting—but in that moment, you are experiencing growth and expansion. This card shows a tall stone tower being struck by lightning, knocking the crown from its position on top. Two terrified figures leap from the flaming building toward an uncertain landing. The tower itself represents the structural foundation that your life is built upon, while the crown is symbolic of ego being shattered by the lightning bolt of illumination. This powerful card tells us that falling apart is a necessary step in our journey, allowing the next phase to arise in its place. The Tower swiftly tears down old structures that no longer support growth.

UPRIGHT KEY MEANINGS
Upheaval, sudden change

REVERSED KEY MEANINGS
Hanging on, fear of letting go

NUMEROLOGY
1 + 6 = 7. Connected to The Chariot (7), referencing the relationship between control and change.

ASTROLOGY
Mars (aggression, outward action, masculine energy)

GENERAL READING

The Tower signals sudden changes that are beyond your control, causing you to feel momentarily destabilized. The message this card offers is that you must persevere, since the aspects of your life that are being torn down are no longer serving you. There is a new way of thinking and being that wants to break through. These new structures will support your growth and expansion.

LOVE/ROMANCE

This card indicates the breaking down of existing patterns in relationships, leading to a change that will support stronger bonds and new ways of partnering. The old ways no longer serve you.

CAREER/MONEY

Sudden change in matters of money can be unnerving, but what you're experiencing now will lead to a breakthrough, a loss clearing the path to greater gain. Tearing down existing structures prepares you to align with a new career path or way of earning money.

PERSONAL/SPIRITUAL

Breaking down old structures makes way for a new way of being in the world. Sudden upheaval or change leads to new levels of illumination on your path. You may see new ways of looking at the world and the weakness of the structures around you. Change is possible.

REVERSED

The reversed Tower card in your reading can indicate that the effects of this card are more subtle, and less devastating. It may also indicate that you're making attempts to avoid what is happening, clinging to an old way of being or doing things instead of facing inevitable change. The Tower wants you to know that it is safe to accept what is happening even if it feels uncomfortable, and that you should trust you are being led where you are meant to go.

REFLECT ··

→ What aspects of your life are changing suddenly or violently, evoking the Tower?

17 ✳ THE STAR

The Star lights the path to healing by pouring the light of the cosmos onto the earth.

....

A renewed sense of hope and healing are brought by the Star card. It shows a woman kneeling on a riverbank, with one foot in the water, symbolizing her connection to spirit and the earthly realm. Stars in the sky look down to guide her as she pours from two pitchers, one onto the land, the other into the water, referencing the unconscious, hope, renewal of faith, inspiration, and creativity flowing from a divine source. The Star represents all that is possible when you allow healing energy to flow into your consciousness, leading to greater healing in both the physical body and the spiritual self.

KEY UPRIGHT MEANINGS
Hope, healing

KEY REVERSED MEANINGS
Loss of faith, disconnection from source

NUMEROLOGY
1 + 7 = 8. Connected to Strength (8).

ASTROLOGY
Aquarius (futuristic, visionary, intelligence)

GENERAL READING

The Star appears to lift your spirits after a time of painful or violent transformation, and she helps renew your faith and hope in the future. Allow this card to inspire you to get back into a state of creative flow by utilizing all of the gifts you have within you. Healing energy is present, both in body and spirit.

LOVE/ROMANCE

Healing from a prior relationship or within a current one is in process now, so have faith in your romantic life. Trust that your path to love is guided and protected, and that the difficulties of the past are behind you.

CAREER/MONEY

You are being guided toward opportunities to advance in your career. Creative ideas for financial improvements are flowing toward you, so be open to flashes of inspiration. This card may also indicate that you are healing from a monetary or job loss.

PERSONAL/SPIRITUAL

You are healing from the past and feeling hopeful for the future. Divine inspiration is flowing toward you, so allow yourself to act on your creative impulses. The near future holds improved health, as well as positive growth, in the realms of spiritual and physical well-being.

REVERSED

The reversed Star in your reading symbolizes a disconnection from the divine, urging you to reconnect. Do not lose faith in the process; you are still on the right path. Inspiration is on the way, so don't give up. Your body and soul will heal, but that healing will take time.

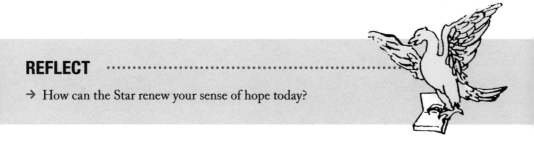

REFLECT

→ How can the Star renew your sense of hope today?

18 ✳ THE MOON

The Moon illuminates what has been hidden, bringing it into the light and asking you to listen to your intuitive messages.

The Moon card is an invitation to confront your shadow self or the dark elements of your essential being that are often suppressed. Your shadow self is not to be feared but rather embraced and integrated. Doing this allows you to heal what you deem unlovable or unacceptable in yourself. On this card, we see a coyote and a dog howling at a full moon, symbolizing our discomfort with duality and the unknown. The coyote is the wild self, while the dog represents our domesticated self. A crayfish in a river symbolizes the quest for the meaning of life, looking deeper, and feelings of dissatisfaction with living a surface existence. The Moon is positioned between the two towers first shown on the Death card, representing the conscious and the unconscious. Under the light of the moon, all is revealed. This includes the messages received in dreams and through intuition. What is revealed may show you where you have been deceived, most likely by your own perceptions. It is time to see the truth and situations clearly.

UPRIGHT KEY MEANINGS
Dreams, illusions

REVERSED KEY MEANINGS
Bypassing difficulties, refusing to acknowledge the truth

NUMEROLOGY
1 + 8 = 9. Connected to The Hermit (9).

ASTROLOGY
Pisces (intuitive, empathetic, self-sacrificing)

GENERAL READING

The Moon reveals aspects of your shadow self, illuminating your dark, self-defeating, and negative traits. This card presents the duality of human nature in its most primal form, as well as highlighting the urge for evolution. By opening yourself up to expanding your consciousness, you are forced to see what has been previously hidden. Do you want to evolve along your spiritual path or remain in the dark, where it feels safe? The Moon shows you where the work can be done, through dreams and developing your intuition. Even in the dark, there is nothing to fear!

LOVE/ROMANCE

You may not have seen something clearly in the relationship, but now the truth comes to light. Secrets are revealed, leading to honest conversations. It may mean confronting your own truths in your relationship or before entering into one.

CAREER/MONEY

Listen to your intuition and read all contracts carefully, as you may unearth hidden fees or discover that a deal is too good to be true. You may have to examine any reasons within yourself that prevent you from achieving your goals or growing into a position of authority at work.

PERSONAL/SPIRITUAL

Now is your time to examine self-deception, fear, and shame by working with your shadow self. Exploring psychic development and dream work can help you reconnect to aspects of your inner self that have been hidden. You are evolving and expanding your consciousness on your spiritual path.

REVERSED

The reversed Moon in your reading may point to a refusal to acknowledge the truth or resistance to looking deeper when your intuition has been asking you to do so. It may also point to overcoming self-deception, so trust your intuitive guidance and gauge where you are on your spiritual journey.

REFLECT •

→ What may the Moon illuminate for you?

19 ✳ THE SUN

The Sun reveals a clarity that comes only after we have spent time with the darkest parts of ourselves.

....

The Sun signifies great clarity and the enthusiasm that comes after emerging from the darkness. An infant, arms open wide, rides on the back of a white horse beneath the bright sun, both representing the return of innocence, optimism, and freedom. A red flag flies nearby, symbolizing renewed passion and the presence of love. The sun itself looms on the horizon, huge and vibrant, representing the card's main message of clarity and illumination. A field of sunflowers in the distance reminds you that life blooms once again, and so will you. There is a sense of relief in this card and a reminder that every dark night has a new dawn.

UPRIGHT KEY MEANINGS

Clarity, optimism

REVERSED KEY MEANINGS

Pessimism, confusion

NUMEROLOGY

1 + 9 = 10, 1 + 0 = 1.
Connected to The Magician (1)
and Wheel of Fortune (10).

ASTROLOGY

The sun (life-force energy,
vitality, visibility)

GENERAL READING

Seeing the world through the eyes of a child, or connecting to your own inner child, is a rewarding and productive use of this card's energy. The Sun offers clarity in murky situations and brings you the experience of renewed vitality and conscious understanding. Improved health is on the way, as well as a return of your enthusiasm for life.

LOVE/ROMANCE

This card signals renewed passion and love in an existing relationship, or a bright future with a new love on the horizon. The Sun is about having fun and being playful in romance. It may also accompany news of pregnancy or the desire to start a family of your own.

CAREER/MONEY

Exciting new opportunities are about to present themselves. Alternately, you may be feeling renewed optimism and enthusiasm for your current job or business. If you are an entrepreneur, keep your mind open to new ideas for business models or revenue generation. Working with children or a family business could bring you immeasurable joy.

PERSONAL/SPIRITUAL

You are feeling healthier inside and out after overcoming a period of sadness or illness. Consider pursuing some inner-child healing work, perhaps by finding a new passion or engaging in a hobby you once loved.

REVERSED

The Sun is one of the only cards in the deck that means virtually the same thing whether it is drawn upright or reversed. Sometimes it can be difficult to recognize that things are changing when shifts don't happen overnight, but the reversed Sun can ask you to take a second look at your circumstances and celebrate the small wins. They add up in time, if you are attuned to them. Beware of being pessimistic, because things are improving.

REFLECT

→ After a period of darkness, what is the Sun illuminating for you right now?

20 ✳ JUDGMENT

Judgment serves as the ultimate release when we are accepting of the past and of ourselves as we follow the divine call to our spiritual awakening.

••

You are ready for the next step in personal growth: accepting yourself and releasing the past. In the Judgment card, an angel in the sky blows a trumpet while people emerge from caskets, rejoicing as they heed the call. The artwork on this card references the biblical resurrection on Judgment Day. Overt Christian themes aside, what you see on this card is a depiction of answering the universe's signs that prompt a spiritual awakening. During the awakening process you reflect on your life, choices, actions, and experiences. As you judge yourself, remember to have compassion for who you once were, and release those judgments so you are able to move on from the past.

UPRIGHT KEY MEANINGS

Awakening, acceptance

REVERSE KEY MEANINGS

Self-doubt, resentment

NUMEROLOGY

2 + 0 = 2 (and 1 doubled, or 11). Connected to The High Priestess (2) and Justice (11).

ASTROLOGY

Pluto (transformation, death and rebirth, power)

GENERAL READING

The process of releasing judgment of yourself is important, whether or not a spiritual awakening is taking place. In order to move forward in life, you have to be willing to accept and release your past so you are able to enjoy the next phase of life, whatever it may hold. Judgment contains all the elements of the cycle of surrender-release-forgive, which, taken together, allows you to move on from the past and into a more vibrant future.

LOVE/ROMANCE

Accept your mistakes, as well as those of your partners, so you can successfully let the past go. Past loves may be returning for possible reconciliation, allowing you to make peace with the past and find closure. Seek forgiveness in order to move forward.

CAREER/MONEY

Don't allow past mistakes or decisions in the realms of finance and career to define you. Instead, focus on releasing the past and moving into a new, more successful period. Heed signs from the universe, and follow them toward a new career path or opportunity in business.

PERSONAL/SPIRITUAL

Put your energy toward noticing the signs from the universe so you can begin releasing yourself from self-criticism and judgment. This is the time to start accepting your spiritual gifts, moving on from past pain, and embracing a new period of spiritual awakening.

REVERSED

The reversed Judgment card in your reading can suggest repeating patterns without learning the important lessons. Perhaps you have been judging yourself harshly or clinging to the past, and either of those behaviors will keep you from moving on. This card in reversal can also signify that you are ignoring a higher calling, so do not be afraid to embrace growth and change.

REFLECT

→ Judgment asks: what have you come to accept about yourself?

XXI

THE WORLD.

21 ✳ THE WORLD

A cycle is complete, but the end is also a new beginning. Rejoice as the World rewards you for your hard work.

You are ready to receive the rewards that come from completing the journey of the Fool, which culminates in the World card. The figure on the World card holds a wand in each hand, like the Magician, symbolic of what has been created. A wreath encircles her, indicating victory and success. You'll notice similarities to the Wheel of Fortune card. A wreath is shown floating in the clouds, and the symbols of the fixed zodiac signs—Aquarius (air), Leo (fire), Taurus (earth), and Scorpio (water)—are once again present, indicating these signs and elements were part of the hard work you put into completing this cycle. You will not go through a difficult time and come out empty-handed. Celebrate the rewards that come from completion.

UPRIGHT KEY MEANINGS
Successful completion, reaping rewards

REVERSED KEY MEANINGS
Incomplete action, delayed celebration

NUMEROLOGY
2 + 1 = 3 (it also connects to 1 & 2, or 12). Connected to The Empress (3) and The Hanged Man (12).

ASTROLOGY
Saturn (responsibility, restriction, time)

GENERAL READING

The World signifies the end of a cycle and reminds you that when you complete a project, you experience the rewards of your efforts. Celebrate your wins, and acknowledge how far you've come. There is excitement around what is yet to come, and you are now ready to begin a new journey from a place of empowerment and maturity.

LOVE/ROMANCE

You are actively celebrating your love and feeling fulfilled in your relationship. You may also be learning lessons and moving into a new phase of your relationship, all while feeling confident and excited for the future.

CAREER/MONEY

You may soon be receiving rewards or recognition at work in the form of a promotion or raise (or even graduation!), as a way of celebrating your success. Consider taking on more responsibility and rising to the occasion in your career.

PERSONAL/SPIRITUAL

You have completed one phase of life that will propel you into the next. Celebrate where you are now and take time to think about how far you've come. You have reached your goals and can revel in feeling proud of yourself.

REVERSED

The reversed World card in your reading is a message that a cycle is ready to be completed, even if you are not quite ready to accept this. There may be a lack of closure or a delay in the gratification from your efforts that prevents you from seeing a situation has come to an end. If this is the case, know that closure is something you can offer to yourself by affirming you're ready to move on and open up to a new energetic cycle, trusting you have grown and are ready for the next adventure to begin.

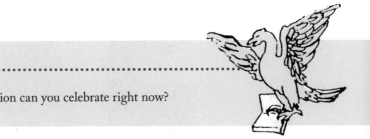

REFLECT ······································

→ What cycle of completion can you celebrate right now?

CHAPTER 5

Minor Arcana: Cups

....

EACH OF THE four suits in the tarot depicts its own elemental journey. The Cups represent the elemental suit of water and the water signs in astrology: Cancer, Scorpio, and Pisces. Cups are symbolic of emotions, feelings, love, and intuition. Beginning with the Ace of Cups, we will explore the universal meanings of each card. An easy way to remember that cups are associated with emotions, love, and feelings is to think about the phrases "my cup runneth over," "you can't pour from an empty cup," and "is the glass half full or half empty?"

....

ACE *of* CUPS

The gift of new love is presented; be open to receiving this gift from the divine.

....

The Ace of Cups signals the gift of a new beginning rooted in love and emotional experience. The hand of the divine emerges from a cloud, offering a golden chalice—the cup of love—from which five streams of water flow into a blooming lily pond. The streams of water tell us that the cup's influence can manifest in many different ways in our lives. A white dove symbolizes peace, and the wafer in its mouth represents a gift of connection to the divine.

UPRIGHT KEY MEANINGS

New love, relationships

REVERSED KEY MEANINGS

Depletion, disappointment

NUMEROLOGY

1, new beginning, the individual

GENERAL READING

When the Ace of Cups appears, the divine is offering you the love gift, which can arrive in many forms, including self-love, a new relationship, or a new connection that will bring love, peace, and happiness into your life. Be open to receiving this gift; it was meant for you!

LOVE/ROMANCE

New love is coming! Taking time to focus on loving yourself helps bring more love into your life. If you are already partnered, you may experience a renewal of love and emotional outpouring within an existing relationship. This card can also signify pregnancy, or the arrival of a new baby.

CAREER/MONEY

A new opportunity or job is on the horizon, and it will be emotionally fulfilling. Alternately, you may be enjoying your current work with renewed enthusiasm. New sources of income from creative endeavors may present themselves soon.

PERSONAL/SPIRITUAL

Focus on self-love and taking time for yourself. New opportunities and inspiration for personal development will appear for you soon. You will soon feel increased enthusiasm for your spiritual practice.

REVERSED

The reversed Ace of Cups in your reading can signify feeling empty or depleted and in need of self-care. It may also indicate feeling disappointed by a relationship that did not work out as planned. Ultimately, when the Ace of Cups is reversed, look within to nourish yourself emotionally.

REFLECT

→ What gift is being presented by the Ace of Cups?

TWO *of* CUPS

*The meeting of two brings balance and
harmony in a nurturing relationship.*

....

This card indicates that you are ready to
take an existing connection to a deeper
level. The Two of Cups depicts two
figures—closely resembling the High
Priestess and the Fool—gazing into one
another's eyes as they exchange cups.
Between them, a winged lion sits atop a
caduceus, the lion symbolizing passion
and protection from above, the caduceus
evoking balance in communication. The
garlands on the heads of each figure represent mutual victory in this harmonious
partnership. The house in the background
references a peaceful domestic life.

UPRIGHT KEY MEANINGS
Partnership, union

REVERSED KEY MEANINGS
Disharmony, breakup

NUMEROLOGY
2, partnership, balance

GENERAL READING

The Two of Cups symbolizes shared feelings and mutual attraction. The partnership may be romantic, with both parties sharing a connection that runs deeper than mere physical desire. Whatever form this relationship takes, there is nurturing energy present and a dynamic of equal give-and-take.

LOVE/ROMANCE

A wonderful new relationship is on the way, or is just beginning. Alternately, your current relationship is filled with love, mutual support, and emotional fulfillment.

CAREER/MONEY

A new partnership or work opportunity is coming into alignment for you. In existing career circumstances, you should experience equal give-and-take in work relationships or an act of generosity from a coworker.

PERSONAL/SPIRITUAL

Deepening your spiritual practice or diving into a hobby will lead to new connections based on mutual interest. In current relationships, you are reveling in feeling loved and supported in your life.

REVERSED

The reversed Two of Cups in a reading can indicate the presence of disharmony or imbalance in a relationship. It can also signify a new or pending breakup, which is always painful and difficult. Try to remember that by saying "no" to certain relationships, you are creating space in your life for more fulfilling relationships.

REFLECT

→ What do you think the two figures are offering one another in the Two of Cups?

THREE *of* CUPS

*Rejoice and celebrate with the people
you care about and allow your
connections to lift your spirits.*

....

A card evoking joyous expansiveness,
the Three of Cups depicts three maidens
dancing together in a garden, their cups
raised in a toast. Drawing this card means
you are celebrating friendship, community,
and all of life's communal pleasures. The
lush, ripe vegetation signifies enjoying life
in the present moment, while the three
maidens represent connection, fertility, and
creativity.

UPRIGHT KEY MEANINGS

Celebration, togetherness

REVERSED KEY MEANINGS

Feeling emotionally drained,
overindulgence

NUMEROLOGY

3, community, creativity

GENERAL READING

The Three of Cups urges you to have more fun, be playful, and focus on spending time with friends or family. Connecting with others is a great stress reliever and rejuvenates your spirit. Indulge in the activities that feel expansive and joyous, surrounded by people who uplift and inspire you.

LOVE/ROMANCE

Drawing this card indicates you could meet a new partner through friends. It also serves as a reminder that love comes into your life when you're doing what you love and enjoying yourself. If you're already in a relationship, get out and have some fun with your partner, especially in a group or in community with others!

CAREER/MONEY

Now is a great time to collaborate with people who support you. This type of compassionate connection helps empower you to feel safe in taking on new projects, knowing you have a strong team to back you up. Bonding with coworkers or making friends with people who work in your industry will lead to new opportunities.

PERSONAL/SPIRITUAL

You are craving time with your soul family! Prioritize connecting with a community that supports you and lifts your spirits. Celebrating with good friends or family is what you need most right now.

REVERSED

The reversed Three of Cups in your reading can point to overindulging or partying too much, so perhaps you've been socializing too often and are feeling drained of energy. It can also indicate tension in friendships, gossip, and boundary issues. Sometimes this card can even point to an affair. Allow your intuition to guide you to what feels true for you.

REFLECT

→ What is your connection to your community, friendships, and creativity?

FOUR *of* CUPS

Looking at the past will not show you your future. Opportunities are everywhere, if you shift your gaze to see them.

Stagnation and boredom loom large in the Four of Cups card. A young man sits under a tree, his arms and legs both crossed, while the hand of the divine emerges from a cloud, offering him a cup. The cup appears to be right in front of him, yet his eyes are downcast, gazing numbly at the three other cups in front of him. His body language is closed off from receiving anything, showing that he's protecting himself from feeling vulnerable. He cannot see a glowing new opportunity because he is too focused on the cups in front of him. These cups represent the past, situations that were unfulfilling in some way. He wants to experience fulfillment, but he doesn't seem to know how to move on.

UPRIGHT KEY MEANINGS

Apathy, stagnation

REVERSED KEY MEANINGS

Refusal to change, stuck in a bad mood

NUMEROLOGY

4, restructuring, reframing

GENERAL READING

It can be challenging to shift your perspective and get excited for something new when you've been hurt or disappointed in the past. Will the next experience just be more of the same? Will you get your hopes up for nothing? These are the types of questions posed by the Four of Cups. Like emotions, water needs to flow freely, and in this card emotional energy is stagnant. In an effort to protect yourself from experiencing pain, you've begun to restrict yourself from feeling anything, which leads to apathy.

LOVE/ROMANCE

There are new opportunities for love and romance in the air, so shift your focus from the past to the unlimited possibilities of the future. Staying stuck on previous loves blocks new energy from flowing into your life, even within current relationships. Open up, even if it feels scary. It's time to let people in!

CAREER/MONEY

You may be bored with your current job, or disenchanted by your current position.

Changing your attitude or making moves to shift your outlook can radically alter your circumstances. This change begins with you, so be sure to notice how doors start to open when you take control of your feelings.

PERSONAL/SPIRITUAL

This card serves as a gentle confrontation over outdated mindsets, or aspects of your spiritual practice aren't lighting you up the way they used to. The Four of Cups tells you it's time to open up to something new. Cultivating willingness to move on from the past automatically opens new doors for you.

REVERSED

The reversed Four of Cups is very similar to its upright meaning yet carries an even deeper attachment to the past. Dissatisfaction with your current situation cannot be solved by focusing on past events or replaying old stories. Don't wait for your outer situation to change; change begins from within.

REFLECT

→ Why do you think the figure in this card is refusing the cup being handed to him?

FIVE *of* CUPS

Focusing on what has spilled will only take you so far. Move through melancholy to find your way to acceptance.

....

On the Five of Cups, a figure stands in a black robe, indicative of mourning, his head bent in sorrow. Before him, three spilled cups suggest loss, heartbreak, and sadness. There is a river that separates him from the buildings and trees, representing physical isolation and distance. Behind the figure are two upright cups, as well as a partially obstructed bridge. If he could only turn around, he would see all is not lost; not only are there still cups standing, there is another way for him to get back to civilization. The journey may take a while, but he will get there.

UPRIGHT KEY MEANINGS
Grief, sadness

REVERSED KEY MEANINGS
Silver linings, moving on

NUMEROLOGY
5, challenge, struggle

GENERAL READING

The Five of Cups asks you to acknowledge your feelings of sadness and disappointment. Go ahead and cry it out! The grieving process takes time, but it will not last forever. The two standing cups will be full again as you make your way out of darkness and rediscover joy, connection, and satisfaction. There is always a way out.

LOVE/ROMANCE

Feelings of disappointment or sadness may surface in your relationship. You also may be overwhelmed by feelings surrounding a breakup or loss of a relationship. Allow yourself a mourning period before reconnecting to love; there is always hope.

CAREER/MONEY

A job or business venture that did not go as hoped has created feelings of loss or grief surrounding work and money. Disappointment in your career is weighing you down, but these feelings are a turning point. A new career direction or partnership is on the horizon.

PERSONAL/SPIRITUAL

The grieving process is necessary for you to move into your next emotional phase of life. Isolation, sadness, and depression should be acknowledged and treated with compassion. Have patience with yourself.

REVERSED

The reversed Five of Cups in your reading is a hopeful sign, showing that you have turned a corner in how you perceive your situation. Seeing the silver lining and accepting the truth puts you on the path to healing and growth.

REFLECT

→ When was a time you felt the sorrowful energy of the Five of Cups?

SIX of CUPS

*A loving exchange of support
and care feels like home.*

After a period of grief or hardship, you've crossed the bridge into the harmonious energy of the Six of Cups card. A young boy and girl, dressed up like storybook characters, appear to be playing in the main square of a sunny yellow town. The boy hands a cup with a white flower to the little girl. The two are surrounded by white flower–filled cups, symbolic of innocence. The children, their silly costumes, and the mood of playful innocence all evoke childhood memories and a desire to spend time where you grew up. There is a figure in the background carrying a spear who seems to protect the children while they play. They are safe and free of worry.

UPRIGHT KEY MEANINGS
Harmony, memories

REVERSE KEY MEANINGS
Nostalgia, living in the past

NUMEROLOGY
6, harmony, reciprocity

GENERAL READING

The Six of Cups asks you to remember when you felt safe, carefree, and playful. Spending time with children, if you have them, or reconnecting to your own inner child are great ways to connect to this card's power. Alternately, find ways to spend time with old friends or people who feel like family. Tapping into the joy you felt as a child will help you make the most of the present moment, either by offering you support and love or by helping you reconnect with your youthful spirit.

LOVE/ROMANCE

You are in a loving, supportive relationship that feels like home or involves children. Now is a great time to consider taking a partner home to meet your family. If you aren't currently partnered, you may meet someone who you can open up to about your past.

CAREER/MONEY

Working with children feels really good for you. Having the support of your family, or feeling like your coworkers are a family, motivates you to focus and achieve. Try to nurture feelings of harmony and support at work.

PERSONAL/SPIRITUAL

Spending time with your children and connecting to your own inner child will refresh you. Playful creativity and the acts of giving and receiving loving support will bring great harmony to your life. Consider spending time with old friends or friends who feel like family.

REVERSED

The reversed Six of Cups in your reading can point to an unhealthy attachment to nostalgia, or a belief that the past was somehow better than the present. Are you wishing things were the way they used to be instead of embracing the possibilities that lie before you?

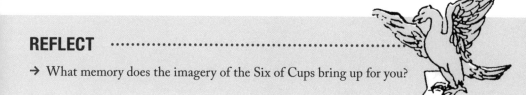

REFLECT ··

→ What memory does the imagery of the Six of Cups bring up for you?

SEVEN of CUPS

If you can dream it, you can achieve it. Just make sure you understand your choices and have a solid plan before you act on your emotions.

Imagining endless possibilities is the activity depicted in the Seven of Cups card. A figure marvels at seven cups that appear to be emerging from clouds, much like those shown on the Ace of Cups and Four of Cups. Are these gifts from the divine, or are they the earthly dreams of the figure who views them? Each cup contains a different dream, including wealth, victory, love, wisdom, passion, fantasy, and power. The figure must carefully consider the cost of these dreams, and what it would take to make them real.

UPRIGHT KEY MEANINGS
Possibilities, daydreaming

REVERSED KEY MEANINGS
Illusions, confusion

NUMEROLOGY
7, planning, contemplation

GENERAL READING

The options presented in the Seven of Cups represent dreams that have not yet materialized. Before a desire can come into form, it exists as energetic potential, as you see in the cups in this card. Which cup do you want to focus on? If you meditate and look within, your intuition will lead you toward what is most resonant as you consider all possibilities.

LOVE/ROMANCE

Your love life may be crowded with too many choices, and you're feeling a need for clarity around your heart's true desires. The relationship you're seeking is available, but you must put energy toward identifying it. Only then can you follow your intuition toward making it a reality.

CAREER/MONEY

So many big ideas! Inspiration and dreaming for the future are the first steps toward creating a fulfilling career. Pick one thing to focus on and follow your intuitive guidance toward the next steps. Check in with your gut feelings about business offers to make sure they resonate with you.

PERSONAL/SPIRITUAL

Take some time to sit with your dreams; practice stepping into them through visualization or guided meditation. Use elements of your spiritual practice to guide you in your decision-making, helping you choose with your heart.

REVERSED

The reversed Seven of Cups in your reading can warn that appearances are often deceiving. This is a reminder to beware of things that seem too good to be true. Be careful not to go all-in on something that causes extreme emotions, since that feeling of intense excitement can vanish as quickly as it arrived. Look to see the underlying truth of each situation and proceed with caution.

REFLECT

→ What daydreams would you like to transform into realities?

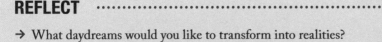

EIGHT of CUPS

Never settle for "good enough." The best option awaits you when you seek it.

....

After wrestling with disillusionment and false promises, the Eight of Cups card shows that you're finally ready to walk away from trying and counterproductive situations. Beneath a crescent moon and watchful sun—representing the conscious self and intuitive self—a figure walks away from eight cups. He is clad in a red robe and boots, symbolic of passion grounded in desire. This person has sampled each cup and decided that none of their contents are satisfying, so he must go off in search of deeper fulfillment. The staff he carries reminds us of the Hermit's staff, a symbol of power, which he leans on for support as he follows the path of the flowing river. The river symbolizes intuition and feeling his way forward in the dark, navigating the path by the light of the moon.

UPRIGHT KEY MEANINGS

Walking away, moving on

....

REVERSED KEY MEANINGS

Hanging on, avoiding change

....

NUMEROLOGY

8, movement, transition

GENERAL READING

The Eight of Cups is a reminder that you do not have to settle if you sense that there is something missing in your life. You don't need to know exactly what you are missing, though you must be willing to follow your heart and instincts toward a more meaningful existence. In order to make that journey, you will need to release things that once brought you happiness, including people, behaviors, objects, and places. This may feel distressing in the moment, but don't let that flash of sadness trap you in a situation longer than you need to be. The inner call to action awaits you.

LOVE/ROMANCE

You are walking away from a relationship that no longer serves you. This may mean leaving behind a pattern of behavior that does not serve your current relationship, or cultivating detachment from unhealthy relationships in the future.

CAREER/MONEY

You're ready to abandon a job or career path that is no longer fulfilling. You've been feeling mentally checked-out, and now you need to take action by leaving a job, career, or project that isn't in line with your goals and ambitions.

PERSONAL/SPIRITUAL

Walking away from friendships and associations that are not aligned with your personal beliefs or spiritual path can be hard but necessary. You're setting out in search of deeper meaning in your life, either through travel, through a spiritual practice, or by looking inward.

REVERSED

The reversed Eight of Cups in your reading can serve as a gentle reminder that you've stayed in a relationship, job, or situation longer than necessary. Perhaps you fear change, but now is the time to walk away. There is something better for you, so trust in the unknown.

REFLECT

→ What do you suppose the figure is feeling as he walks away from the cups?

NINE *of* CUPS

*Sit back and revel in the abundance
you've cultivated, as gratitude
increases the flow of success.*

....

The Nine of Cups card brims with the
energy of abundance, wealth, and security.
Here we see a proud-looking man seated
with nine cups displayed like trophies
behind him. He's worked hard for these
cups, and he is pleased with his accomplishments, as indicated by the blue cloth
beneath them. The Nine of Cups carries the
energy of each card that came before, experiencing each lesson along the road. Known
as "the wish card" in the tarot, this card
signals fulfillment of your dreams or efforts
coming to fruition.

UPRIGHT KEY MEANINGS

Satisfaction, abundance

REVERSED KEY MEANINGS

Overindulgence, arrogance

NUMEROLOGY

9, nearing completion, solitude

GENERAL READING

The Nine of Cups asks you to relax and enjoy what you've worked hard to achieve, and don't downplay your successes. You've come a long way, all on your own, and your abundance overflows. Savor these moments, share your good fortune with others, and your generosity will always flow back to you.

LOVE/ROMANCE

A new level of happiness and intimacy is reached, either within an existing relationship or a budding one. You are attracting a partner who is happy and fulfilled within themselves and ready for a serious relationship. Love and happiness overflow.

CAREER/MONEY

Current projects are reaching completion, so look forward to celebrating before moving on to welcome a new idea. You may expect to receive recognition for a job well done, or even a promotion. Following your intuition and honoring your ideas will lead you to increased prosperity and abundance.

PERSONAL/SPIRITUAL

Your health is improving, and you're welcoming overall feelings of happiness and joy. Make a wish and continue to follow your intuitive guidance on your path. This card signals abundance in all areas of life.

REVERSED

The reversed Nine of Cups in your reading may reveal arrogance surrounding achievements and needing constant validation and recognition. It can also point to overindulging in life's pleasures and needing to implement moderation. When you consider the abundance in your life, celebrate it by expressing gratitude and generosity.

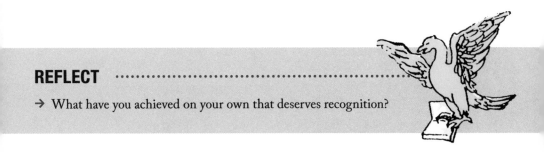

REFLECT ···

→ What have you achieved on your own that deserves recognition?

TEN of CUPS

The culmination of emotional fulfillment
is the gateway to the next adventure.

∙∙

A celebratory card filled with the energy
of completion, the Ten of Cups indicates
you've reached an apex of emotional fulfillment. On it, a happy couple stands in an
embrace, with their free arms outstretched
as they welcome ten shining cups that have
appeared in a rainbow above them. Their
two children dance beside them, and a
river runs through the lush landscape they
inhabit, leading to a house on top of a hill.
This couple has it all, including love, a happy
family, and a safe home. They are grateful
for their prosperous life.

UPRIGHT KEY MEANINGS
Happiness, fulfillment

REVERSED KEY MEANINGS
Disharmony

NUMEROLOGY
10, a complete cycle

GENERAL READING

Emotional fulfillment looks different to each individual at different stages of their life, so consider what it means for you. It may manifest as a happy family or a wonderful community that feels like a family. The Ten of Cups focuses on achievement of a level of love and success that fills your life with serenity, satisfaction, and gratitude.

LOVE/ROMANCE

You may already be in a relationship built on mutual love and respect, but a focus on supporting one another is needed for you to take the next steps together. Happiness within the family or a relationship involving children may be front and center right now, or you may be getting along with your ex if you share custody of children.

CAREER/MONEY

You're experiencing both success in the workplace and success in the home. Enjoy the feeling of a happy work/life balance, and acknowledge any support you receive from your coworkers that feels like family. If you're eager to start a business or make a positive change in your career, know that you have the support of your family or the people around you.

PERSONAL/SPIRITUAL

Longstanding family issues are nearly resolved, or you may be headed for a family gathering that will bring everyone closer together. Enjoy the sensation of feeling secure with your overall well-being, and make time to celebrate your success with people who feel like family. You're well on your way to achieving a big milestone goal—in your career or love life—propelling you toward your next phase with increased stability.

REVERSED

The reversed Ten of Cups in your reading can indicate a delay in or an obstacle to achieving security, conquering a big goal, or creating harmony within your family dynamic. There may be a disconnect between you and a partner or family member, but as with any reversal, you have the opportunity to turn this situation around. Be patient and listen to your heart to get back on track.

REFLECT

→ What does emotional fulfillment look like to you?

PAGE of CUPS

PAGE of CUPS.

The messenger of love brings good news;
be open to new emotional experiences.

Pages are considered to be the messengers in the tarot. The Page of Cups card's youthful energy may represent a child or younger person in your life, or perhaps a message from your own inner child, urging you to have more fun. The young Page in this card wears a fancy floral tunic and flowing scarf around his head. Hand on hip, he gives a playful look to the fish that emerges from the cup in his hand. There is an element of flirtation, mystery, and playfulness between these two. The Page stands on land as water flows behind him, representing the double elements of earth and water indicated in this card.

UPRIGHT KEY MEANINGS

Love messages, playfulness, emotional intelligence

REVERSED KEY MEANINGS

Immaturity, oversensitivity

ELEMENTAL KEY COMBINATION

Earth & water. Earth signifies the Page's connection to nature and stability, while his place within the suit of Cups gives him a connection to water, which represents love and flowing emotion.

GENERAL READING

The Page of Cups is grounded in his identity and feels free to express himself. This card signals emotional intelligence and messages in your life that praise you for actively expressing your feelings. The Page could represent another person, or he could be you. Regardless, open yourself to receiving messages from unexpected sources, including your own intuition.

LOVE/ROMANCE

News of new love is coming to you. If you're feeling flirtatious and romantic, share your feelings with a partner. Focus your energy on having more fun, experimenting with creative dates, and trying new activities with your love interests.

CAREER/MONEY

An exciting new opportunity is on the horizon. Take it slow, but put yourself out there in a way that feels emotionally satisfying. Your finances are improving, and you're becoming more confident at work, even if you still feel like a novice sometimes. Relish the moments that make you feel like a beginner, enjoying the incredible lightness that comes with it.

PERSONAL/SPIRITUAL

Get in touch with your inner child by finding playful ways of expressing yourself. Listen to your instincts about any messages or inspiration that flows into your life now. If you choose to begin new creative projects, approach them with the curiosity of your inner child. Learn to find awe in small moments.

REVERSED

The reversed Page of Cups in your reading can point to feeling unable to fully express yourself. You may be taking life too seriously and not making time for joy, play, or being present in the moment. This card can also serve as a gentle confrontation that asks you to be more sensitive to others' feelings. Have you shown carelessness or immaturity recently, or realized that you're taking things too personally?

REFLECT

→ How can you find more ways to incorporate playfulness into your daily life?

KNIGHT *of* CUPS

The quest for love brings speedy results that may or may not stand the test of time. Pace yourself.

· ·

Knights are depicted on horseback, returning from a noble quest to present you with the item you requested. The Knight of Cups rides in on a white horse, proudly offering up the prized cup. The wings on his helmet and feet show the Knight's connection to the element of air, while his place in the suit of Cups connects him to water. The horse indicates the speed of time it has taken the Knight to return from his quest. Air and water move quickly, indicating hasty emotional decisions being made without careful consideration.

UPRIGHT KEY MEANINGS
Emotional offerings, speed

REVERSED KEY MEANINGS
Perfectionism, disappointment

ELEMENTAL KEY COMBINATION
Air & water. Air signifies the Knight's connection to communication and the mental realm, while his place within the suit of Cups gives him a connection to water, which represents love and flowing emotion.

GENERAL READING

Consider the motivations behind gestures, including your own actions. Are you doing something purely for recognition and attention? It is easy to get swept up in emotional experiences, such as idealizing someone or something. Slowing down will allow you to see the person or situation more clearly and enjoy the process as it unfolds.

LOVE/ROMANCE

The ideal partner is coming into your life, but take things slow while enjoying the romance. Alternately, you may experience renewed romantic feelings in your relationship, possibly including a proposal or declaration of love. You are either acting on romantic feelings or preparing to do so.

CAREER/MONEY

Offers, new projects, or challenging assignments get you excited for your work again. A new boss or coworker offers you some much-needed support. If you're feeling stagnant, open your mind to the inspiration you need to make work more enjoyable for you.

PERSONAL/SPIRITUAL

Good news is on the way that will help you feel optimistic regarding your health. You may have uncovered a new source of inspiration on your spiritual path. A new addition to your home feels exciting—possibly a pet, furnishings, or a roommate.

REVERSED

The reversed Knight of Cups in your reading can signify disappointment within a relationship, especially if your high hopes and expectations were not met. Perhaps a promising new romance fizzled out too quickly, or the object of your desire turned out to be different from how they'd first appeared. This card in reverse can also indicate that you're relying too heavily on your desire for perfection in yourself or another. Adjusting expectations of yourself and of others—and forgiving everyone for their shortcomings—can help you get back into a more positive emotional state.

REFLECT •••

→ What aspect of your life is causing you to rush?

QUEEN of CUPS

The feminine energy of love, nurturing, and protection resonate within the Queen of Cups.

Queens in tarot represent feminine energy that includes receptivity, creativity, nurturing, and love. The Queen of Cups is entirely emotional, carrying the double element of water. She feels deeply, expressing her emotions and wearing her heart on her sleeve. We see the Queen seated on a throne decorated with shells and baby mermaids, signifying her connection to maternal instincts and ability to create life. The throne is surrounded by water, so she truly is in her element. The golden crown on her head suggests her connection to higher consciousness, and she gazes at a covered chalice in her hands, intuitively protecting its contents.

UPRIGHT KEY MEANINGS

Nurturing, feminine energy

REVERSED KEY MEANINGS

Suspicion, emotional distance

ELEMENTAL KEY COMBINATION

Water & water. Water is connected to the Queen's nurturing and loving energy, and her place within the suit of Cups means she offers a double dose of love and emotional outpouring.

GENERAL READING

The Queen of Cups can represent an actual person in your life who embodies these characteristics, including yourself, but this card can also symbolize the energetic presence of intense emotions in your life. Ask yourself: Is there someone who has been influencing my emotions? Have my own emotions been trying to tell me something? When I look within, what messages do I receive about nurturing myself?

LOVE/ROMANCE

This card may represent a wonderful romance with a loving, nurturing, compassionate partner. Do not be afraid of vulnerability in your relationships, as they are signs of emotional intelligence that lead to deeper connection. Listen to your heart and heed your intuition, since trusting yourself will lead you to experience greater love. The Queen of Cups also carries indications of motherhood, children, and family.

CAREER/MONEY

Using your intuition in the workplace reveals new opportunities. Be open and receptive to creative inspiration that's coming your way. You may notice an outpouring of nurturing support for a specific project or increased supportiveness from someone in your workplace. You are creating something you care about, so protect your ideas while letting them breathe and grow.

PERSONAL/SPIRITUAL

Focus on developing your intuitive abilities. Activities like dream analysis and journaling about messages you receive in dreams can help you become more in tune with your inner self. Spend as much time as you can with people who inspire you, and embrace activities that allow you to be more creative. You may also find joy in spending time at home, nesting, redecorating, and putting your love into everything you do.

REVERSED

The reversed Queen of Cups can indicate jealousy or envy that you are feeling or that someone else is feeling of you. It can also point to feeling suspicious or cautious of others. This card may be asking you to open up about your feelings without worrying about being rejected or judged. If there is someone in your life who has proven themselves untrustworthy, a healthy disconnection may be necessary.

REFLECT

→ What would the Queen of Cups ask you to nurture in yourself?

KING of CUPS.

KING *of* CUPS

Masculine energy of taking action from a place of compassion and love are upheld within the King of Cups.

....

In tarot, Kings are the masters of their suit, representing stability, authority, and healthy masculine energy. The King of Cups represents the elements of fire and water, which exist in harmony without overpowering one another. The King is seated on a concrete throne that appears stable despite floating in water. The ship in the background symbolizes taking action for himself but also on behalf of the many passengers aboard. He is able to navigate emotional depths without allowing the waves to drag him downward. Many people rely on the king, and he is loving, empathetic, and intuitive in response to their needs.

UPRIGHT KEY MEANINGS
Emotional stability, empathy

REVERSED KEY MEANINGS
Unreliability, lack of boundaries

ELEMENTAL KEY COMBINATION
Fire & water. Fire signifies the King's connection to action and leadership, while his place within the suit of Cups gives him a connection to water, which represents love and flowing emotion.

GENERAL READING

The King of Cups can represent a person who embodies the qualities of empathy, compassion, and emotional intelligence and takes action to uphold their boundaries while being mindful of those around them. That person may be you! This card can also represent the energy of a situation that requires the setting of boundaries and expression of compassion.

LOVE/ROMANCE

You are blessed by the presence of a partner who is stable, sensitive, and emotionally intelligent. It may take a little time to open up to one another, but once the walls come down, there is wonderful potential for deep love. Bring the energy of compassion, empathy, and support into your relationship in order to deepen your connection.

CAREER/MONEY

You are moving into a leadership role at work, or others at work view you as a leader. You may be organizing people around a cause or an event. This card indicates that you are already in a stable career or are capitalizing on a wise financial investment opportunity. Listen to your gut rather than overanalyzing or intellectualizing in the workplace, since this will lead you toward positive outcomes.

PERSONAL/SPIRITUAL

You are working on creating or maintaining strong boundaries in your relationships. Allow yourself to rely on the presence of support and emotional stability through tough times. It may also mean that you are in a position to support others and provide guidance. Others may look to you for leadership in a creative project.

REVERSED

The reversed King of Cups can indicate shaky boundaries or emotional instability, within you or around you. Be careful about who you rely on for support, and be aware that you may need to dig deeper into your own reserves instead. It may also mean that you doubt your own ability to lead while others are looking to you for guidance. There may be confusing communication in the near future, leading to hurt feelings or feeling rejected by someone who is just not able to open up fully. Try not to take it personally.

REFLECT

→ How do you see yourself in the King of Cups?

CHAPTER 6

Minor Arcana: Pentacles

· ·

THE PENTACLES REPRESENT
the elemental suit of earth and the earth
signs in astrology: Taurus, Virgo, and
Capricorn. Pentacles are symbolic of money,
the physical body, nature, stability, and
all things abundantly tangible. An easy
way of remembering that pentacles are
associated with money, health, and stability
is to think about the phrase "money doesn't
grow on trees," yet money is made of paper,
and paper comes from trees! The idea of
"planting seeds for future growth" is another
reminder of the earth element. Also consider
stability and how feeling stable in your body
is called being "grounded." For many of
us, feeling stable in the world is linked to
having an adequate amount of wealth.

· ·

ACE of PENTACLES

A prosperous new beginning is unfolding for you. Be open to receiving gifts from the divine.

The Ace of Pentacles bears the gift of a new beginning, rooted in the element of earth. Here we see the hand of the divine reaching through the clouds to offer a golden coin with a pentacle on it. Beneath the coin there is a beautiful garden with lush flowers blooming, a symbol of great abundance and prosperity. Here, in the garden, you have everything you need to ensure success. Take what you need as you venture beyond the floral archway and out into the world, trusting that you have planted seeds that will take root and ground you through any of life's challenges.

UPRIGHT KEY MEANINGS

New beginnings, abundance

REVERSED KEY MEANINGS

Delayed abundance

NUMEROLOGY

1, new beginning, the individual

GENERAL READING

The Ace of Pentacles signifies an opportunity or gift from the universe in the material realm. That may come as a new job or unexpected sum of money. Since this card is about beginnings, it could also indicate that you're taking the first steps toward increasing prosperity and cultivating greater abundance for yourself. This change has unlimited growth potential, so grab ahold and see where it takes you!

LOVE/ROMANCE

A new love is coming into your life, or you are in the beginning phases of a significant relationship that will become stable and grounded. You may feel the urge to take an existing relationship to a new level of commitment through a shared decision, such as buying a home together. Now is a time of increased abundance and stability in your love life, so relax and enjoy the bounty.

CAREER/MONEY

A new job, raise, or opportunity will soon present itself that will pay off in terms of increased income and stability. Real estate and new property are favored if you have been searching for a new office space. You are ready to pursue a new career path that will offer more stability and abundance.

PERSONAL/SPIRITUAL

You are following a new path of self-care and wellness that leads to vibrant health. Keep an eye out for new opportunities to create stability and wealth, such as an inheritance or generous gift.

REVERSED

The reversed Ace of Pentacles in your reading indicates there is an opportunity presenting itself that you are unable to see. Perhaps this is because you're trying too hard to make something work, or you are heading in the wrong direction. The universe is asking you to loosen your grip and relax your need for control. Open yourself to divine assistance! You may not recognize what is right in front of you, since it doesn't look like what you've been imagining.

REFLECT ·······················

→ What gift is being presented by the Ace of Pentacles?

TWO *of* PENTACLES

Achieving balance is possible when you focus on prioritizing what is most important.

You are at a point in your personal development where you feel ready to integrate important life changes and achieve the sense of balance shown by the Two of Pentacles card. The figure in this card is holding two pentacles connected by an infinity loop, signifying that one directly affects the other. He stands on one foot as he attempts to balance these two energies. Behind him, two ships navigate turbulent waters, representing the struggle to find stability amidst emotional upheaval.

UPRIGHT KEY MEANINGS
Balance, stability

REVERSED KEY MEANINGS
Tension, irresponsibility

NUMEROLOGY
2, harmony, balance

GENERAL READING

Balancing your schedule and personal obligations can be tricky. The Two of Pentacles asks you to flow with your emotions rather than allowing them to wash over you and knock you off balance. Anytime you strive to take your life to the next level, your routine and comfort zone will be momentarily disrupted. This is a normal part of expansion, but to leverage it in a healthy way, you will need to take a moderate approach. Only take on what you can handle, and reach out for help when you feel overwhelmed.

LOVE/ROMANCE

Balancing a relationship with your schedule can get off track when love is so fun. Enjoy your romance, but make sure you're taking time for everything and everyone else. You may soon face a choice between two relationships, or realize that juggling multiple partners is causing you to neglect your responsibilities. Strive for balance while you enjoy your romantic life.

CAREER/MONEY

Put your energy toward managing your finances or balancing your budget to maximize your money. You may need to choose between your current job and your side hustle or passion project. Strive to find a good balance between what you put into your career and your home life. In other words, don't spread yourself too thin at work!

PERSONAL/SPIRITUAL

You may be struggling to find the right balance for yourself between your social life and your work life. Choosing between what you are passionate about and what you think you should be doing can be challenging. Trust that you will be able to handle all aspects of your life despite any unexpected challenges.

REVERSED

The reversed Two of Pentacles in your reading can indicate tensions in your life that leave you feeling unbalanced or destabilized. It may indicate that you aren't being responsible with your money or that you're spending unnecessarily when you should be saving. These challenges are momentary, and balance can be easily restored by identifying where you are off track and taking small steps to get back into alignment.

REFLECT ·····························

→ Where in your life do you need more balance?

THREE *of* PENTACLES

Prosperous expansion is at your fingertips as you confidently walk through new doors of opportunity.

You've already worked to create balance in your life and are now ready for the expansive opportunities presented by the Three of Pentacles card. Here we see three people gathered in lively conversation, collaborating on a plan that will change their lives for the better. The man standing on the bench is the craftsman; he has valuable expertise and is confidently standing above the other two figures, explaining his vision. Three pentacles carved into the architectural detail show that this collaborative work is stable and long lasting.

UPRIGHT KEY MEANINGS
Success, new doors opening

REVERSED KEY MEANINGS
Burnout, lack of confidence

NUMEROLOGY
3, collaboration, expansion

GENERAL READING

The Three of Pentacles asks you to share your ideas with confidence and accept projects and work that stoke your passions. Your work will not only be well-received by others, it will position you to open new doors of opportunity. This is the next level of prosperity you have been waiting for, so do not doubt your abilities and skills. You have what it takes to build the prosperous future of your dreams.

LOVE/ROMANCE

Put yourself out there despite feeling intimidated. Spend time with people who inspire and motivate you, since this places you in a position to make a romantic connection through friends. Existing relationships are going to grow and flourish through expansive projects, either creative or home-related.

CAREER/MONEY

Your career is about to present you with new opportunities. Apply for the job that scares you, let people know you're available, or take steps toward starting your own business. Now is the time for you to shine.

PERSONAL/SPIRITUAL

Increased confidence amidst fears leads you to grow and expand in many ways. Consider working on your skills at public speaking or becoming visibly active within a community. Establishing your presence and growing your audience in your field of expertise will lead to fulfillment.

REVERSED

The reversed Three of Pentacles in your reading can suggest a lack of confidence or overwhelming fear of taking your work to the next level. It's time to step out of your comfort zone if you are serious about growth. You may also be feeling burned-out from work, so remember that taking a break won't hurt your career. Allowing yourself to rest will reenergize you, so don't push yourself so hard.

REFLECT

→ What would life feel like if you took more risks and allowed yourself to dream bigger?

FOUR *of* PENTACLES

Holding too tightly to the material world will never satisfy your need for a sense of security.

....

The doors of abundance are opening all around you, but now you must reevaluate your relationship to resources and stability. In the Four of Pentacles, we see a man surrounded by abundance, wearing a crown and sitting upon a throne. Despite having all the things he needs, he appears uncertain about the lasting quality of his good fortune. One coin sits atop his crown, indicating that money is always on his mind, while he clutches another coin to his heart, showing he is emotionally tied to his wealth. Finally, the remaining two coins are under his feet, showing us that his sense of stability is directly tied to how much wealth he has. With so much emphasis on needing to see the physical manifestation of stability, there is very little room to create more abundance through generosity and opening up to the unlimited creative powers of the universe.

UPRIGHT KEY MEANINGS
Building stability, conserving resources

REVERSED KEY MEANINGS
Materialism, controlling behaviors

NUMEROLOGY
4, structure, creating stability

GENERAL READING

Feeling financially stable is a concern for everyone, and once you've achieved some level of comfort it's easy to focus on maintaining what you've got and lose sight of potential growth. The Four of Pentacles asks you to affirm that you are stable and safe, and remember that you will always have what you need. Conserve what you've earned without closing yourself off to new paths to abundance. You have or are in the process of establishing stability for yourself, so give yourself some credit for your hard work.

LOVE/ROMANCE

You, or a partner, are waiting until you feel more established before making a more serious commitment such as buying an engagement ring, buying property, or starting a family. Careful planning isn't sexy, but a sense of stability is needed before either of you feels comfortable in taking the next steps.

CAREER/MONEY

Financial security is motivating your career choices rather than passion or creativity. You've opted to take on a traditional role or be conservative with your money and investments. In your current position, you're waiting for physical proof rather than acting on intuitive guidance in matters of business.

PERSONAL/SPIRITUAL

Your natural gifts are abundant, so don't focus merely on matters of money in order to feel stable. If you are saving for the future or a specific goal, you're being very conservative with your resources. This card serves as a reminder to be generous, since giving to others brings more prosperity into your own life.

REVERSED

The reversed Four of Pentacles can show that you've been focusing too much on the material side of life. Emotional and mental stability are just as important as material stability, though you won't see the tangible results in your bank account. Insecurity cannot be cured by amassing wealth and possessions. It's time to focus inward rather than outward. This card can also indicate that you are being too controlling across the board and need to relax. Listen to your intuition; what does your gut tell you to do to guide yourself back into balance?

REFLECT •••

→ Which resources do you tend to cling to?

FIVE *of* PENTACLES

Focusing on your fears won't bring abundance into your life. Shift your attention to feeling abundant, and watch as your circumstances change before your eyes.

With the Five of Pentacles card, you're asked to examine your faith in the abundant universe during challenging times. The two people featured on this card appear impoverished and physically suffering as they trudge through the snow. They walk past a beautiful stained-glass church window depicting a tree with five golden coins, representing a warm spiritual sanctuary offering charitable care. Yet these two do not feel worthy of that charity and are determined to walk stubbornly toward further decline.

UPRIGHT KEY MEANINGS
Focusing on lack, feeling physically or financially depleted

REVERSED KEY MEANINGS
Moving on from challenges

NUMEROLOGY
5, challenge, difficulties

GENERAL READING

The Five of Pentacles indicates feelings of lack and loss, and fear of scarcity. These emotions may have been caused by a job loss or some set of circumstances leading to a lack of resources. When you focus on what you lack, it can be difficult to see that assistance is close at hand. When you move from a mindset of needing to "see it to believe it" to one of "believing it before seeing it," abundance is created within you. Your feelings of worthiness combined with faith in the divine can lift you out of any period of loss.

LOVE/ROMANCE

Losing a relationship is destabilizing, and this can make it difficult to open up and trust a new partner. But in order to experience love in all of its abundance, you must move through your worries about instability. A relationship that is on shaky ground may leave you fearful or doubting yourself, but have hope that a resolution can be reached, even if that resolution is an end to the relationship itself.

CAREER/MONEY

You are grappling with fears around losing a job or general financial instability. This card may represent an actual job loss or something less concrete, but regardless of the details, your fear-based actions are actually leading you toward something that suits you far better. Have faith in what is coming, even if you feel uncomfortable in this moment. You will have what you need.

PERSONAL/SPIRITUAL

Shift your focus from the material world toward the spiritual world in order to handle fears about stability and resources. Creative solutions will appear when you ask for divine guidance. Health concerns may be looming in your life right now, but focus your mind on healing instead of suffering.

REVERSED

The reversed Five of Pentacles in your reading can indicate that you are moving away from the financial challenges you've experienced but have lingering fears about falling back into hardship. Focusing on your spiritual practice or simply choosing to have faith that your situation is changing will give you the boost you need to release feelings of lack and loss.

REFLECT

→ What is one way you handle feelings of scarcity?

SIX *of* PENTACLES

Giving and receiving opens the flow of prosperity in your life. Always give what you would like to receive.

You are met with generosity and even exchange when you draw the Six of Pentacles. In this card, a wealthy man offers coins to people who are kneeling before him. His body position is above theirs, yet he holds a scale in his hand as a reminder that equality is important, as is sharing what you have with those who have less. This card is as much about giving generously as it is about receiving graciously. Altruistic and genuine acts of support are the hallmarks of this card.

UPRIGHT KEY MEANINGS
Generosity, sharing resources

REVERSED KEY MEANINGS
Generosity with strings attached, inequality

NUMEROLOGY
6, harmony, generosity

GENERAL READING

The Six of Pentacles asks what is your relationship to giving and receiving? Giving offers its own reward in the good feelings that flow from being generous. Receiving can sometimes leave you feeling unworthy or undeserving, especially when you do not have anything to offer in return. Don't feel obligated to give back to the same source you've received from, since they are already satisfied with the act of giving. Instead, remember these moments of kindness, and give to others when an opportunity arises. The more comfortable you become with receiving, the more abundance will flow into your life.

LOVE/ROMANCE

A relationship based on genuine care and equal give-and-take is here for you or on its way. A generous partner or gift is coming to you, so be open to receiving it. Now is a perfect time for sharing and connecting deeply within a relationship.

CAREER/MONEY

A generous offer, windfall of money, or abundant return on an investment is on its way. You are getting back what you've put into a project and feeling great about it. Keep your eyes open for a raise or promotion, but also consider helping someone at work who needs resources or financial support.

PERSONAL/SPIRITUAL

An inheritance or unexpected gift is coming to you, or you are considering donating to charity or someone in need. Consider passing along items from your closet or home to those in need, since doing so will create space to receive from other sources.

REVERSED

The reversed Six of Pentacles can come as a warning of generosity with heavy strings attached, or a warning to watch out for intentions behind the act. This may relate to you giving with an expectation of getting something in return, and being disappointed. Try to give your time, energy, and resources to people and situations where the only reward you can expect is the joy of being of service.

REFLECT

→ How can you be more giving today?

SEVEN of PENTACLES

You need to tend to your garden, knowing it is abundant and will feed you for years to come, before you see the fruits of your labor.

This card demands that you be patient while you take small steps to nurture your work. The Seven of Pentacles indicates that a project, idea, or relationship you've been nurturing is not yet fully formed. The man on this card is shown leaning on his gardening tool, looking at his crop of pentacles. He's been working for a long time, carefully tending to its growth. By pausing to look at what he's accomplished, he sees that he has not reached his goal and feels frustrated rather than proud of himself for how far he's managed to come. The pause is the motivation he needs to refocus and get back to work. He knows in his heart that staring at the beautiful pentacles won't make them grow any faster.

UPRIGHT KEY MEANINGS
Growth, patience

REVERSED KEY MEANINGS
Impatience, procrastination

NUMEROLOGY
7, planning, contemplation

GENERAL READING

You are so close to reaching your goal! Alas, it isn't time to celebrate quite yet. When you pause and look at your progress, do so with gratitude rather than frustration. You're being asked to remember that the journey toward achievement is an adventure, not a destination. How can you enjoy the work you're doing even more? Trust that when the time is right, the fruits of your labor will be perfectly ripe and celebration will be in order.

LOVE/ROMANCE

You may be in a hurry to get to a particular relationship milestone, but try to slow down and enjoy the adventure imbued in this moment. The universe is bringing the right relationship to you at the right time. Be patient and continue to work on taking care of yourself.

CAREER/MONEY

You may be disappointed by where you are in your current job, feeling you should be further in your career, but this is part of the process. Have faith that with continued perseverance you can achieve your goals. Stay patient and continue to dedicate yourself to the hard work you've been putting in.

PERSONAL/SPIRITUAL

You are very close to seeing the tangible results of your efforts, so don't give up now! Your daily self-care or spiritual routine is slowly bringing about the changes you've been hoping for. Stay positive and grateful for the small promises you keep to yourself, since they compound over time.

REVERSED

The reversed Seven of Pentacles in your reading can suggest that you haven't been working toward your goals with enough conviction, and you're getting frustrated and impatient. This reversal can also reveal that procrastination is the main reason why you haven't seen the results you've been hoping for. Overcome any internal resistance by reviewing and revising your action plan. Perhaps your goal just needs a little adjustment to get you back on track.

REFLECT ···

→ What is growing in the Seven of Pentacles that has yet to be harvested?

EIGHT *of* PENTACLES

The only way to become skilled at something is to continually engage in practicing it. Your skills are worth developing.

....

The Eight of Pentacles is all about mastering your chosen craft. The apprentice in this card works diligently to hone his skills. He knows that success is a combination of education and practical application. Neither step can be avoided if he is to reap the financial rewards for his efforts. He is happy to do this work, since he believes in himself and has no problems tackling the same tasks day after day. In his heart, he knows that he is working toward mastery.

UPRIGHT KEY MEANINGS
Hard work, productivity

REVERSED KEY MEANINGS
Burnout, overworking, being undervalued

NUMEROLOGY
8, movement, transition

GENERAL READING

The Eight of Pentacles reminds you that when you do what you love, you will love what you do. Financial success and security are the product of your hard work and dedication, and the level of your success is up to you. If you've been working hard to learn something new or advance within your current field, your efforts will not go unnoticed. Keep up the great work!

LOVE/ROMANCE

Not the sexiest card, but it does indicate a partner or yourself is dedicated to building a stable foundation to grow a relationship and possible family. One of you may be a workaholic, but this is because they want a secure future. Make time to play if that person is you!

CAREER/MONEY

Hard work and dedication are leading you toward increased financial prosperity. If you continue down this path, you will move up the ladder of success, either within a company or by building your own company. Learning and mastering a new skill will increase your income by allowing you to change careers or by opening up a stream of passive income.

PERSONAL/SPIRITUAL

What you have been studying or practicing will lead to abundance. Cultivating your spiritual practice may lead to working in the healing arts. Trust that you can do anything you set an intention toward and that you can achieve success through diligent work that you enjoy.

REVERSED

The reversed Eight of Pentacles in your reading can indicate feeling burned-out. You may be considering leaving your job or feeling uneasy about the career path you've chosen for yourself. Do you feel as though you're working really hard and achieving nothing meaningful? Be honest with yourself when you answer this tough question, and remember that it's never too late to begin again!

REFLECT

→ What passion project does the Eight of Pentacles represent to you?

NINE of PENTACLES

Luxuriate in your prosperity, feeling gratitude for all that you've been able to achieve.

....

The Nine of Pentacles implores you to relax and enjoy the comfortable surroundings you've cultivated for yourself. A woman stands in her garden, serene and unafraid to get her hands dirty despite her lavish flower-printed robe (which is reminiscent of the robe worn by the Empress). She knows how to receive the energies of abundance and is equally suited to putting in any work necessary to tend her home. On her hand sits a bird wearing a hood, a symbol of her instinct to guard against materialism while enjoying prosperity.

UPRIGHT KEY MEANINGS
Success, enjoyment

REVERSED KEY MEANINGS
Materialism, lack of appreciation

NUMEROLOGY
9, culmination, solitude

GENERAL READING

The Nine of Pentacles symbolizes a time of enjoyment and feeling safe. You've worked hard, made intelligent choices with your money, and invested wisely. You also value charity and generosity, making sure to share your abundance with others. It's time to enjoy the world you've cultivated for yourself so meticulously. There is no need to worry about scarcity, since you have everything you require. Go ahead and take a vacation or buy yourself something meaningful; you've earned it.

LOVE/ROMANCE

Focus on your own pleasure without feeling guilty. If you are single, you've been doing a great job loving yourself, but know that there is potential to meet someone who shares your values and will prove to be a solid romantic partner. Do something special for yourself rather than waiting for a partner to make a move. Your sense of value comes from within.

CAREER/MONEY

Financial security is yours, so relax and enjoy what you've achieved. Take a break if you've been overworking, since rest and relaxation will recharge you when you return. Work can wait! You'll still be abundant after a well-deserved vacation.

PERSONAL/SPIRITUAL

You've been putting your energy into making your home more personal and comforting by redecorating or renovating. Or if you've been away from home, you've spent time taking a vacation and relaxing. Focus on what brings you the most peace; enjoyment rejuvenates your spirit.

REVERSED

The reversed Nine of Pentacles in your reading can serve as a gentle reminder regarding overspending or materialistic tendencies. If this resonates for you, rein in your spending and unsustainable financial behaviors. This reversal also may point to overworking and not taking time to enjoy your life, another unsustainable practice. Check in with your intuition to see where your imbalance lies.

REFLECT

→ Which of your achievements makes you feel the most proud?

TEN *of* PENTACLES

The culmination of prosperity has arrived. This enables you to create from a new place of abundance alongside those you love.

....

A card of shared wealth and bounty, the Ten of Pentacles shows three generations of a family enjoying themselves in the luscious garden on their property. The family is surrounded by ten pentacles, showing that they do not have to worry about matters of finance. The two dogs are symbolic of loyalty, while the depiction of children, adults, and an old man illustrates the process of maturing that unfolds throughout your life.

UPRIGHT KEY MEANINGS

Wealth, family, inheritance

REVERSED KEY MEANINGS

Loss, breaking with tradition

NUMEROLOGY

10, complete cycle

GENERAL READING

The Ten of Pentacles represents love within the family that is most supportive in your life, though that may not be your family of origin. Focus on spending time with the people you love and creating a network of prosperity that will give generously to those in need. This may be an inheritance for you, or may mean that you are beginning to set aside funds that will benefit your children, your aging relatives, or a partner. Enjoy the present while planning for this prosperous future.

LOVE/ROMANCE

You are either in or entering a relationship with someone that has long-term potential, including marriage, buying property, building a family, and enjoying old age. This card indicates you seek traditional values, abundant resources, and generosity within a relationship. Now is a good time to take your partner home to meet your family or introduce them to your friends.

CAREER/MONEY

You are considering starting or entering a family business, and you have the support of your family and plenty of resources. You may be entering into a partnership with close friends. Generosity and support are being extended toward you, or you may be offering these things to someone else in the workplace.

PERSONAL/SPIRITUAL

Buying a home or inheriting property or money are all current possibilities. You're also seeing overt generosity from your family or important members of your social circle. You have plenty of love and support to further your dreams, especially when you seek advice from people you respect who are older and wiser.

REVERSED

The reversed Ten of Pentacles can represent a challenging time within the family. You may feel controlled by the expectations of your parents, siblings, or partner, and want to break away to forge your own path. Conflicts over property or disputes in the home may arise. This reversal may even represent a fear of moving to the next level once a place of comfort has been reached, despite your intuition telling you it's time for a change.

REFLECT

→ What does ultimate material success look like for you?

PAGE *of*
PENTACLES

The messenger of prosperity brings news of stability. Stay grounded and enthusiastic in your approach.

....

As one of the messengers of the tarot, the Page of Pentacles brings youthful energy and may represent a child or younger person in your life, or a message from your own inner child, urging you to plant seeds of forthcoming prosperity. Standing in a beautiful field, this Page proudly gazes at the pentacle in his hands. His green tunic and natural surroundings reference his connection to the earth, while his eyes are fixed on his pentacle, showing he has a vision and is focused on achieving his goals.

UPRIGHT KEY MEANINGS

Manifestation, solid beginnings

REVERSED KEY MEANINGS

Procrastination, lacking
a solid plan

ELEMENTAL KEY COMBINATION

Earth & earth. Earth signifies the Page's connection to nature and stability, and his place in the suit of Pentacles also connects him to earth, so this Page offers a double dose of practicality and grounded effort.

GENERAL READING

The Page of Pentacles may be a novice or someone working to establish himself in a new place or new profession. This card may represent working at the beginning stages of a project or starting down a new path. What you are working toward is grounded in reality and can grow into lasting abundance with focus and steady effort. Be open to receiving messages from a variety of sources, especially your own intuition.

LOVE/ROMANCE

A new relationship is blooming that has the potential to be stable. This partner may be in the early stages of personal achievement, focused on achieving their goals. Putting effort into building a solid foundation is a worthwhile use of your energy. This card may be more practical than romantic, but it indicates that your romantic life is centered on someone stable and trustworthy, or finding someone with those qualities.

CAREER/MONEY

You are encountering prosperous new beginnings in the workplace, an investment opportunity, or a new business idea—all of which require careful planning. You may be developing a new career interest, skill, or income stream. You've been working with focus and are making steady progress. Take action on your ideas without rushing.

PERSONAL/SPIRITUAL

This may mean you're beginning a new creative project, health routine, or wellness practice. Stay steadfast in your vision and know that the beginning stages can often be frustrating. Listen to your intuition to guide you to the next practical steps to propel yourself forward.

REVERSED

The reversed Page of Pentacles can address procrastination around important goals and asks you to refocus or readjust your approach if you want to see results. This reversal may also suggest frustration around a lack of progress in reaching your goal or a desire to jump ahead to the finish line. If you're pouring your energy into a project or effort that isn't turning out as you'd hope, it may be time to look elsewhere.

REFLECT

→ What new path are you considering embarking upon?

KNIGHT *of*
PENTACLES

*The quest for prosperity moves slowly
and steadily. True success is a long
game, so don't rush the process.*

Knights in the tarot are depicted on
horseback, returning from a noble quest
to present you with an elemental item that
you requested. The Knight of Pentacles is
the only Knight in the tarot whose horse
appears to stand still, which highlights his
connection to the earth element. His horse
is black to evoke a sense of protection. His
careful contemplation of the pentacle in
his hand symbolizes his connection to the
element of air, the element of intellect. This
Knight knows that in order to bring you the
abundance you've requested, he will need
to exercise patience and make intelligent
choices. He is assured prosperity because he
pays attention to details and is methodical in
his actions.

UPRIGHT KEY MEANINGS

Long-term abundance,
steady progress

REVERSED KEY MEANINGS

Hesitation, complacency

ELEMENTAL KEY COMBINATION

Air & earth. Air signifies
the Knight's connection to
communication, while his
place in the suit of Pentacles
connects him to earth,
which represents stability
and connection to nature.

GENERAL READING

The Knight of Pentacles isn't impressed by get-rich-quick schemes or lazy short-cuts. He understands that putting in solid effort daily will yield the most lasting and meaningful results. This is true for your mundane daily tasks as well. Showing up fully and enthusiastically in all areas of your life—not just for things you are passionate about—creates abundance in many ways. Set goals and take realistic action steps to avoid burnout, and your routine will transform into a successful daily practice.

LOVE/ROMANCE

As a partner, the object of your affection may not be the exciting or flashy type, but they are stable, grounded, and trustworthy. More sensual than passionate, this person takes things slow. Together you are creating a relationship that is built on trust and stability rather than excitement and intensity. That said, you will need to take things slow if you want the relationship to last.

CAREER/MONEY

An investment you've made appears to be moving very slowly, but be patient! It will yield prosperous results if you let it unfold organically. Continue to take steady action on your goals while remaining patient and realistic about your expectations. If you're searching for a job or considering a career change, stay optimistic, since it may take a while to line up the perfect opportunity.

PERSONAL/SPIRITUAL

Taking daily action in small significant ways toward your personal goals or wellness routine is your best bet right now. Soon you'll begin seeing positive changes in your health or bank account. Remember to rely on stable friends or family members when you need support.

REVERSED

The reversed Knight of Pentacles can show hesitation to take action. This reversal may also indicate unhealthy complacency in a job or relationship, causing stagnation. Tune into your intuition and ask yourself where you can make positive changes to redirect your energy and get back into the flow.

REFLECT ·

→ What would you like the Knight of Pentacles to offer you?

QUEEN *of* **PENTACLES**

Feminine energy of nurturing and dependability, as well as a strong connection to nature, are held within the Queen of Pentacles.

Queens in tarot represent feminine energy that includes receptivity, creativity, nurturing, and love, connected to the element of water. This Queen is deeply connected to nature and the element earth, as shown by the beautiful flowers and vines surrounding her throne. She has a healthy relationship with her body and follows her instincts when making decisions. She is grounded, dependable, responsible, and wise. The Queen of Pentacles holds her pentacle lovingly. She gazes at the pentacle as well as beyond it, toward the earth itself. Her feet are firmly planted on the ground, and she knows that her unlimited resources should be shared by everyone.

UPRIGHT KEY MEANINGS
Generosity, dependability

REVERSED KEY MEANINGS
Materialism, unreliability

ELEMENTAL KEY COMBINATION
Water & earth. Water signifies the Queen's connection to love and emotions, while her place in the suit of Pentacles connects her to earth, which represents stability and connection to nature.

GENERAL READING

The Queen of Pentacles can represent a person who embodies these characteristics, including yourself, or the presence of dependable, nurturing energy in your life. Ask yourself questions about the quality of supportive people in your life, your relationship with your body, and how you can connect with nature to feel abundant.

LOVE/ROMANCE

This card may represent a romantic partner who is nurturing, reliable, sensual, and dependable. It may also be telling you that you bring these qualities to a relationship, or it may describe the relationship itself. Trust that these qualities are necessary if you want to build a strong, lasting partnership. Drawing this card may also signify motherhood, fertility, and starting a family.

CAREER/MONEY

Support from someone you look up to—such as a boss, mentor, or life coach—will help move your career forward. You are making positive strides toward your goals, listening to your intuition, and making wise choices. Never doubt that you have full support from your family or close friends, who are dedicated to helping you feel empowered in your career success.

PERSONAL/SPIRITUAL

The Queen of Pentacles may be asking you to examine your relationship with your mother figure, mother your inner child, or connect with the children in your life. This card indicates you should take good care of your body, focusing on wellness and spending time in nature. Caring for your home, cooking, or gardening will help you relax.

REVERSED

The reversed Queen of Pentacles can indicate overemphasis on the materialistic aspects of life and a need to balance them by getting in touch with your spiritual side. It also may point to someone in your life who has become unreliable. Instead of getting angry, have a conversation with them about expectations and make adjustments where necessary. This reversal can also point to someone who has too much influence over your decision-making process. Perhaps you are trying to please someone at the cost of your own happiness.

REFLECT ··

→ What is your connection to nature and its abundance?

KING of PENTACLES

Stable and grounded, the masculine energy of taking action with authority and generosity is embodied by the King of Pentacles.

....

Kings are the masters of their suit, representing stability, authority, and healthy masculine energy. The King of Pentacles embodies the elements of fire and earth, which exist in harmony without overpowering one another. This King wears a fancy printed robe covered in juicy grapes ripe on the vine and a crown adorned with flowers. His throne sits in his luscious garden, while behind him we see a partial view of his magnificent castle. He has everything he needs and enjoys his luxury, while also providing for the people who live and work in his castle.

UPRIGHT KEY MEANINGS

Wealth, generosity

REVERSED KEY MEANINGS

Greed, self-centeredness

ELEMENTAL KEY COMBINATION

Fire & earth. Fire signifies the King's connection to passion, action, and leadership, while his place in the suit of Pentacles connects him to earth, which represents stability and connection to nature.

GENERAL READING

The King of Pentacles can represent a person with financial stability, generosity, and drive. That person may be you! It can also represent the energy of a situation requiring you to take a leadership role, make financial decisions on behalf of others, or take action reaching a goal. It may require you to use your resources for the benefit of others.

LOVE/ROMANCE

This card may represent a financially prosperous and generous partner coming into your life, or an existing partner/relationship reaching a new level of financial maturity or responsibility. If the latter is the case, you may feel ready to take the next steps toward creating a home or family together. The King of Pentacles evokes a relationship where you both can relax and enjoy security and prosperity. You can celebrate this shared happiness by taking a vacation or splurging on a gift that pampers you both.

CAREER/MONEY

Increased financial success and stability are within your grasp. A partner or investor is coming in to assist you in achieving your goals. It can mean you will be using your resources, such as providing network connections to others or serving as a mentor to someone looking to get into your field.

PERSONAL/SPIRITUAL

You are feeling healthy masculine energy within yourself or around you, perhaps through a supportive father figure, your own internal father figure, or the father of your children. You're looking for ways to be more generous with your resources, whether it's funding causes based on your passions or spending more time with people in need.

REVERSED

The reversed King of Pentacles can indicate someone who is greedy or only focused on material wealth. This can be a father figure or just you being hard on yourself, pushing forcefully to see results. Perhaps you are butting heads with someone who only cares about outer appearances or indulges in self-centered behaviors. Look beneath the surface to see the truth. You may be struggling with your own ability to be generous, to part with the resources that you've built.

REFLECT ⋯⋯⋯⋯⋯⋯⋯⋯⋯⋯⋯⋯

→ Where can you be more generous with your resources?

CHAPTER 7

Minor Arcana: Swords

···

THE SWORDS REPRESENT the
elemental suit of air and the air signs in
astrology: Gemini, Libra, and Aquarius.
Swords are symbolic of thoughts, ideas,
and the words you speak, as well as
written communication. An easy way of
remembering that swords are associated
with communication, thoughts, and ideas is
to think about the phrases "sword of truth,"
"the truth hurts," and "the pen is mightier
than the sword." When someone talks about
you to others, it's called "backstabbing."
There are many examples that compare
swords to various forms of communication,
although many seem unpleasant.

···

ACE of SWORDS

The gift of clarity and new ideas is being presented to you. Be open to receiving this gift from the divine.

....

The Ace of Swords brings you the gift of a new beginning by offering clear insight and new ideas. On this card, we see the hand of the divine emerging from a cloud, offering a single sword with a crown atop it. The crown is symbolic of consciousness and clear ideas that have been received and are ready to be put into action, as shown by the ferns that dangle from it, resembling a wreath of victory. Beneath the hand and sword is a mountain range, representing the ability of the higher self to see far above the ground to receive this divine insight.

UPRIGHT KEY MEANINGS
Clarity, new ideas

REVERSED KEY MEANINGS
Confusion, indecision

NUMEROLOGY
1, new beginnings, the individual

GENERAL READING

When the Ace of Swords appears in a spread, it points to bright ideas, mental clarity, and the instant insight needed for swift action. It may suggest that a new or emerging idea requires immediate action to come to fruition. Diving into an important conversation or a confrontation with someone will lead to a much better outcome. This Ace represents the first exciting step in a process. Trust your intuition to guide you toward the next action steps. This is an encouraging sign!

LOVE/ROMANCE

Don't hesitate to invest in a new relationship or opportunity. Fresh new insight and clarity in an existing relationship will lead to taking action in a positive direction. This card may also signify improved communication in your current relationship or next relationship.

CAREER/MONEY

You are uncovering new ideas for increasing or expanding your business. Clarity and insight on how to improve your money situation are finally emerging. This is a time of new beginnings in your career that may include starting a business or earning a promotion within an existing company.

PERSONAL/SPIRITUAL

Heed the call to deepen your spiritual practice or develop your psychic and intuitive gifts. If you feel struck by inspiration in your personal or spiritual life, take action and don't worry about the details. You will be guided toward the next steps, but to open the portal to that guidance you must be bold and initiate action. You may notice improved communication and clarity with friends and people you spend the most time with.

REVERSED

The reversed Ace of Swords in your reading can suggest confusion or miscommunication. Be active in asking for clarity or more information rather than overanalyzing a situation or interaction on your own. This reversal can also signify feeling defeated, indecisive, or unheard. As difficult as confrontation can be, it's the best way to clear up any hurt feelings.

REFLECT ·····················

→ What gift of clarity is being presented by the Ace of Swords?

TWO *of* SWORDS

Refusal to see the truth not only blocks your intuition, but also prevents any further movement, leaving you trapped in limbo.

....

When multiple options are presented, indecision can prevent you from making a bold choice. The Two of Swords card embodies this inability to commit to a single path. On it, a blindfolded woman is forced to rely on her intuition, since her vision is obscured. She clutches a pair of swords close to her chest, as if to defend herself against pain. Her back is turned to a rocky sea, as if she's pretending it isn't there, but her intuition knows better. She needs to make a decision, but her fear of experiencing pain prevents her from moving forward.

UPRIGHT KEY MEANINGS
Indecision, self-protection

REVERSED KEY MEANINGS
Manipulation, blocked intuition

NUMEROLOGY
2, duality, choice

GENERAL READING

Finding yourself in a place of indecision is just as painful as the fear you experience by choosing inaction. Fear of making the wrong choice will paralyze you, keeping you stuck in a holding pattern. Reaching out and asking for advice and support will help ease your mind, but ultimately, listening to your own intuition and taking action on your own will provide the relief you seek.

LOVE/ROMANCE

Are you ignoring red flags or refusing to make a decision regarding a partner or relationship? You may be forced to choose between two partners or weigh complex options within a single existing relationship. When you avoid conflict or confrontation to avoid risk of pain, you are limiting yourself. Try to release your fears of opening up to love.

CAREER/MONEY

Take time to consider all options before making a career or investment decision. You find yourself feeling indecisive and avoiding financial choices for fear of negative outcomes. Don't hesitate too long; listen to your intuition and choose options that make sense on a gut level.

PERSONAL/SPIRITUAL

You've been protecting yourself from pain due to fears that stem from experiences in your past. Taking time to gather your thoughts before making a big decision is wise, but don't wait too long. If you're feeling indecisive or defensive about making choices in your life, remember that only you know what is best for you. You can make courageous choices if you can only trust yourself.

REVERSED

The reversed Two of Swords in your reading can suggest you have been allowing the thoughts and opinions of others to weigh too heavily on you. This may be preventing you from receiving clear messages from your intuition. In order to reach decisions that are aligned with your true self, turn down the volume of other voices and tune into your own inner monologue.

REFLECT

→ Which challenging life choices are represented by the Two of Swords?

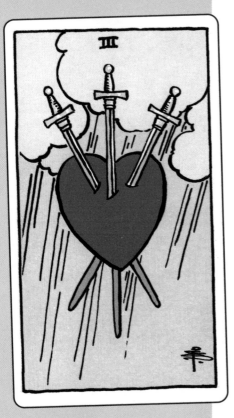

THREE *of* SWORDS

Experiencing pain is a temporary state, but the memory of pain lingers when it goes unacknowledged.

••

In this iconic card, three swords pierce a bright red heart suspended in a stormy sky, as rain falls around it. The swords represent the unkind words, negative thoughts, and painful memories held deeply within your heart. The sky is the conscious atmosphere of the mind, clouded by sadness. The rain, symbolic of tears, points to the importance of releasing emotions and cleansing yourself of these sorrowful experiences.

UPRIGHT KEY MEANINGS
Sadness, pain

REVERSED KEY MEANINGS
Recovery, releasing pain

NUMEROLOGY
3, collaboration, expansion

GENERAL READING

In the Three of Swords, you are given an opportunity to embrace and acknowledge heartbreaking truths and the pain surrounding them. This may be related to a current situation or something in your past that is impacting your present circumstances. If you open your heart and mind, your intuition will guide you toward the meaning of the Three of Swords. Accept your emotions with compassion, and take this opportunity to release and heal. Everything that exits your life creates space for something better suited to your current path.

LOVE/ROMANCE

Heartbreak or disappointment in a past or current relationship is weighing on your mind. Accepting a painful truth or rejection is an important step, as is allowing yourself time to heal and process your feelings. Rejection is redirection; something better awaits you.

CAREER/MONEY

You're coping with feelings of sadness around your career, possibly due to a job loss or disappointing news. This card may also represent arguments with coworkers. Facing a sad truth in the workplace can be uncomfortable, but you must process the loss and allow yourself to heal if you want to move forward in a new direction.

PERSONAL/SPIRITUAL

Leaning on your spiritual practice will help you through times of sadness. Using self-reflection as a method of understanding the lessons behind heartbreak and disappointment will empower you to get more in touch with yourself.

REVERSED

The reversed Three of Swords in your reading is letting you know that, although sadness is present, you are on your way to recovery and releasing the pain that accompanies disappointment and heartbreak. This period of sorrow won't last forever, so look to the future with hope for new experiences. This reversal also serves as a reminder that you should avoid bringing your fear of heartbreak into new situations.

REFLECT

→ What story does your sadness tell? What new story would you like to replace it?

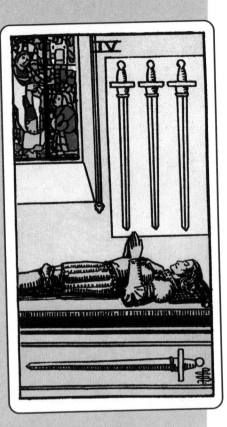

FOUR *of* SWORDS

Pausing to relax and rest your thoughts is a necessary part of life. After this, you'll be able to move forward with greater energy and a clear mind.

You are exhausted from an intense experience, so the Four of Swords asks you to take time to look within yourself, rest, and recuperate. The Knight is depicted as an effigy atop a tomb, yet this card does not signify death. Instead, it symbolizes deep rest. The Knight's hands are clasped in a prayer pose that is used in meditation, yoga, and various religions. The tomb itself evokes silence and time away from the noise of the world. The swords hung on the wall ask the Knight to let his battle weapons rest, while one sword remains beneath the Knight, signifying that he is quick to react when needed.

UPRIGHT KEY MEANINGS

Rest, introspection

REVERSED KEY MEANINGS

Restlessness, avoiding self-reflection

NUMEROLOGY

4, structure, stability

GENERAL READING

The Four of Swords is the recovery period in the journey of the Swords. It asks you to relax, calm your mind, and engage in introspection. If you feel stressed or anxious, meditation and sleep are encouraged. Letting yourself rest creates space within your mind to receive ideas and intuitive messages that lead to solutions. During this time, you can also focus on self-reflection, breath work, and other modalities that calm the nervous system.

LOVE/ROMANCE

Taking a break from dating or stepping back from a relationship can do wonders to bring you closer to someone special. In fact, you may find that you need some time alone to evaluate your priorities and focus on yourself before diving back into the world of love.

CAREER/MONEY

You've been feeling stressed out at work and needing to take a break, or possibly a vacation. Even a small period of time away from the office, such as a personal day, will rejuvenate you. Incorporating stress-management techniques into your daily routine brings increased productivity and a healthier, more sustainable mental state.

PERSONAL/SPIRITUAL

Carving out quiet time to meditate and focus on your spiritual path will do you a world of good. Incorporating more solitude and self-reflection into your life greatly affects your overall happiness and well-being. A card of recovery, the Four of Swords could be related to a period of recuperation from illness or a time of seeking medical treatment, therapy, or counseling.

REVERSED

The reversed Four of Swords in your reading can suggest feeling restless or avoidant of self-reflection and quiet time. You may be opposed to stopping once you've got momentum going, but you must trust that finding inner peace will help you sustain productivity in the long run. This is a warning that you may be teetering on the edge of burnout, and you need to balance your physical/mental output with restorative rest.

REFLECT ·······························

→ What can you do to relax your mind?

FIVE *of* SWORDS

Conflict is unpleasant for everyone, but even if you find yourself on the losing end, you can still walk away with dignity.

There are several levels of struggles buried in the Five of Swords card. A smug young man holds two swords in one hand, while another sword stabs at the earth, and the remaining two swords lie near his feet. In the distance, two figures walk toward the water, defeated and visibly upset. Depicting the aftermath of a battle, this card is heavy with conflict and emotion, signifying conflict and loss, or winning at the cost of destroying important relationships.

UPRIGHT KEY MEANINGS
Conflict, arguments

REVERSED KEY MEANINGS
Releasing, letting go of grudges

NUMEROLOGY
5, challenge, conflict

GENERAL READING

The Five of Swords teaches you that conflict, arguments, and quarreling are a natural element of all relationships, but how you manage yourself during these moments will help you evolve. Start by understanding your triggers. Is it really that important to have the last word? What might these power struggles be trying to teach you? Other times, it's best to know when to walk away from a hostile situation.

LOVE/ROMANCE

An argument or unpleasant conversation needs to be had in order to reach a peaceful resolution. If a relationship or partner leaves you feeling constantly defeated, it is probably time to walk away from it. Sparking arguments with a lover to stir up passion and intensity is an unhealthy pattern. Look for more productive and beneficial ways to experience passion with a partner.

CAREER/MONEY

You may find yourself arguing with coworkers or coping with open hostility in the workplace. Perhaps you're working under a difficult manager who devalues you, leaving you feeling powerless. Know when it is time to walk away from an environment, team, or project that cannot be salvaged peacefully. Listen to intuitive nudges guiding you away from toxic people or a toxic workplace.

PERSONAL/SPIRITUAL

Take time for self-reflection around feelings of anger, and ask yourself what they can teach you about your personal power. Conflicts with family and close friends can help renew those relationships if you dedicate your energy to finding the root of the hostility. Actively addressing hurt feelings often leads to improved communication.

REVERSED

The reversed Five of Swords in your reading can suggest it is time to lay the past to rest and release old grudges in order to move on. Focus on reaching a compromise after a conflict. You may feel intuitively guided to forgive someone and create closure. Even if you do not speak directly to the person, you can set yourself free by forgiving someone in your own mind and heart.

REFLECT ··

→ Is it more important to be right or to maintain peace?

SIX of SWORDS

Moving forward means finding peace in the present while maintaining hope for the future. Trust that the worst is behind you.

. . . .

After conquering a string of conflicts and challenges, you are ready to expand into the serene journey presented by the Six of Swords card. On it, we see three figures with their backs to the viewer taking a boat ride from choppy waters toward more calm waters, heading toward the peaceful shore. The man steering the boat represents masculine, action-oriented energy, while the seated figure is assumed to be female, sitting passively under a hooded cloak. She represents feminine, intuitive energy, while the child sitting nearby may represent the inner child. The six swords standing in front of them inside the boat represent the forward movement of thoughts being safely carried over the water, symbolic of emotions.

UPRIGHT KEY MEANINGS
Moving forward, embarking on a healing journey

REVERSED KEY MEANINGS
Difficulties in moving on, staying in place

NUMEROLOGY
6, balance, harmony

GENERAL READING

The Six of Swords offers a welcome reprieve from conflict, asking you to guide yourself toward release, both mentally and emotionally. This card can be interpreted literally or figuratively, since the action of a healing journey may take place within you or may be tied to a physical journey undertaken to give yourself distance and space. If this card does signal travel, the trip you take will be beneficial for you and an important element of your healing journey.

LOVE/ROMANCE

You may be moving on from a relationship, or a rough patch within a relationship, toward more harmonious times. Consider moving in with a partner, or moving into a new space to expand or begin a family. Better times are ahead for everyone.

CAREER/MONEY

You will soon be leaving a job or situation behind and moving toward much better career opportunities. Positive changes are coming in your finances. A possibility of moving for work is on the horizon; when it presents itself, trust this opportunity.

PERSONAL/SPIRITUAL

You've reached a new level on your spiritual/healing journey, and you are now moving into a period of peace after much struggle. An upcoming move or some travel plans will do wonders for your flagging spirit.

REVERSED

The reversed Six of Swords in your reading can signify a delay or inability to move on from a difficult situation. Ask your intuition to guide you toward issues that still need resolving. This reversal can also indicate that travel plans may be subject to delays. Focus on where you are in the present moment instead of pushing ahead with future plans.

REFLECT

→ If you were a passenger on this boat, where would you be going?

SEVEN *of* SWORDS

Listen to your intuition to help you see what is being taken away from you or hidden from you, right under your nose.

You've just met the notorious thief of the tarot, the Seven of Swords card! A smirking man is in the process of sneaking off while carrying five swords. He appears to tiptoe away from a tent, yet he leaves two swords behind. The yellow background suggests he does this in broad daylight without attempting to hide what he is doing, since yellow represents conscious awareness. Like all swords, these ones represent ideas, thoughts, and forms of communication, so the theft taking place does not necessarily represent a physical object being taken by you or from you.

UPRIGHT KEY MEANINGS
Deception, strategy

REVERSED KEY MEANINGS
Disorganization, paranoia

NUMEROLOGY
7, planning, contemplation

GENERAL READING

The Seven of Swords warns of possible deception and lying. Either someone is being dishonest with you, or you may be lying to yourself about something. This card can also represent a strategy or manipulation tactic you're using to get something you want rather than being open and up-front about your needs. There is always an opportunity to reframe the situation with honesty and frank communication, as suggested by the two remaining swords. So ask yourself what is the Seven of Swords asking you to confront?

LOVE/ROMANCE

Not everything is as it seems. A partner is either lying to or hiding something from you. It may mean you are deceiving yourself regarding the truth of a situation. Now is the time to come clean, be open, and communicate clearly within your relationship.

CAREER/MONEY

Dishonest behavior infects your workplace. Formulate a strategy to get what you want, or leave your job before things get too toxic. If you are indulging self-deception regarding the truth of your finances, it's okay to open up and communicate about money realities.

PERSONAL/SPIRITUAL

You've been keeping aspects of your personal life hidden, but it may be time to open up and have an honest conversation. There's someone in your life who manipulates you, steals your ideas, or wastes your time. Self-deception about the truth of a relationship, situation, or behavior will only lead to more heartbreak.

REVERSED

The reversed Seven of Swords in your reading can signal a plan or strategy that isn't working in your favor and needs to be approached from a different perspective. Don't give up on your idea, just reorganize your thoughts around it and try looking at it from a new angle. This reversal can also indicate paranoia or a misguided belief that someone or something is working against you. Listen to your intuition to separate true gut instincts from the voice of fear.

REFLECT

→ Who do you think those swords belong to, and why is the figure trying to take them?

EIGHT *of* SWORDS

Do not let fear hold you back or keep you trapped in your current reality. With patience and determination, you can always find a way forward.

You are ready to confront some limiting and uncomfortable constraints—including self-imposed ones—when you draw the Eight of Swords card. On it, we see a woman blindfolded and tied up (though not tightly), standing on a watery beach and awaiting the incoming tide. Eight upright swords are planted in the sand around her, while a castle looms in the background. The blindfold suggests she cannot see a way forward and her movement is hindered by her restraints, but the swords are not pointed at her; they merely surround her. This indicates fear of perceived danger or lingering issues from the past holding you back from claiming agency for yourself.

UPRIGHT KEY MEANINGS
Feeling trapped, restriction

REVERSED KEY MEANINGS
Release, hesitation

NUMEROLOGY
8, movement, transition

GENERAL READING

The Eight of Swords indicates you're feeling trapped or stuck, either by circumstances, the past, or your own internal fears of uncertainty. Feelings of separateness, not fitting in, and being unable to express yourself freely are also indicated. You may find yourself making excuses for why you can't move forward or holding everything inside, feeling powerless to spark change. Since the way forward begins when you reclaim your power, start by taking small steps toward your true desires. Have faith and be patient with yourself. This process takes patience and perseverance, but you can do it!

LOVE/ROMANCE

You've been feeling trapped or stuck in a relationship, but giving up and walking away from it feels too daunting. Alternately, you may be battling fears about entering into a relationship or being vulnerable with someone for the first time. The apprehensions are imagined ones, so work on opening up and allowing yourself to experience love.

CAREER/MONEY

You're working a job you don't love and feeling like there's no way out. Or perhaps your fear of failure is preventing you from trying a new career option. Your current money mindset is scarcity-based, which adds another layer of constraint. Remember that you aren't alone; ask the divine for guidance toward steps to take to release yourself.

PERSONAL/SPIRITUAL

You've been feeling trapped in a situation that is no longer in alignment with your path. You know you need to begin to release yourself but aren't sure how. Reach out for help if you feel stuck, and remember that you do not have to struggle alone.

REVERSED

The reversed Eight of Swords in your reading can signify you are in the process of releasing yourself from self-imposed restrictions, so keep going! This reversal may also suggest you've been procrastinating or hesitating to dive into actions that will help you progress. Now isn't the time to stop, or you may find yourself right back where you started.

REFLECT

→ What is holding you back from making meaningful change?

NINE of SWORDS

An anxious mind leads to restless nights. Explore how you handle worry and stress to transform its impact.

A challenging and fraught card, the Nine of Swords opens the floodgates to anxious thoughts and worries that keep you up at night. The figure on this card sits upright in bed, alone in the darkness, as nine swords dangle ominously above her head. Are these swords real? Or are they imagined worst-case scenarios? The blanket that covers her depicts red roses, symbolic of love, showing that there is compassion surrounding her if she would only uncover her eyes and see.

UPRIGHT KEY MEANINGS

Anxiety, worry

REVERSED KEY MEANINGS

Hopelessness, despair

NUMEROLOGY

9, nearing completion, solitude

GENERAL READING

The Nine of Swords is telling you that your anxiety is preventing you from seeing the reality that is in front of you. Stress is a normal part of life, but how you manage it is up to you. If you allow your worries to affect your health and wellness, it is time to make some changes. Implement healthy skills and coping strategies, and seek help if you are struggling. Journaling can help put your thoughts into words and gets them out of your head and onto the page. Fortunately, this negatively charged and counterproductive energy is temporary and will pass.

LOVE/ROMANCE

Conflict is a part of every relationship, even healthy ones. Stressing out about your relationship isn't going to solve the issue, so schedule a conversation with your partner or open up to a trusted friend. Unhappiness can become a cycle, leading to added stress. Worrying about your love life attracts more worry, so do your best to take steps toward finding ways to calm your mind. Communication is key.

CAREER/MONEY

Worry and financial stress are causing loss of sleep or focus. Deep-seated anxiety about your job or career is absorbing too much of your attention. If an overwhelming workload is stressing you out, ask for help without fearing what other people think.

PERSONAL/SPIRITUAL

Stress and anxiety are taking a toll on your physical health. You may be feeling alone or spending too much time ruminating about the same things. Journaling, walking in nature, or spending time with others can help you work through these negative thoughts.

REVERSED

The reversed Nine of Swords in your reading is similar to the upright meaning, but it carries an even deeper tone of despair and may indicate depression or panic attacks. Fortunately, it also points to these cycles ending, so the associated feelings are passing and can be overcome. Be gentle with yourself if you are experiencing extreme anguish and despair, and never be afraid to reach out for support.

REFLECT

→ What tools can you use to break free from anxious and swirling negative thoughts?

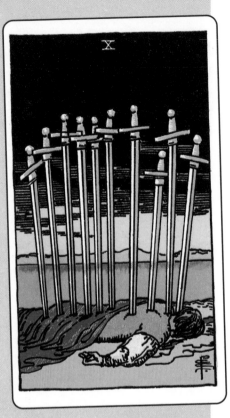

TEN *of* SWORDS

Greet the approaching dawn while honoring lessons learned from the past. There is a new beginning within each ending.

A bright new dawn is depicted in the Ten of Swords card. The darkness of night gives way to a beautiful sunrise, casting its rays onto distant mountains and a body of water that lies between the sun and a man with ten swords in his back. The energies of both death and rebirth imbue this card, reminding us that a cycle of pain nearly always gives way to a new dawn. The man will rise again, but the swords haven't disappeared completely. He is aware of their presence and does not see them as burdens. Rather, he honors the experiences that have shaped his journey and what he has learned along the way.

UPRIGHT KEY MEANINGS

Endings, new beginnings

REVERSED KEY MEANINGS

Delayed endings, hanging on to the past

NUMEROLOGY

10, complete cycle

GENERAL READING

The Ten of Swords signifies the end of a cycle of pain and struggle. Transformation occurs when you accept this ending and allow yourself to see that everything you've experienced has served its purpose. This level of surrender creates a feeling of peace and gratitude for what has left your life, creating space for a new cycle to begin.

LOVE/ROMANCE

The end of a relationship or relationship pattern is leading you toward a wonderful new beginning. Or it may be that a cycle is completing within your current relationship, so it's important to make peace with the past to make way for new energy. In this cycle, the worst is behind you, and you look at that time as a learning period; you look forward to the next phase of romance.

CAREER/MONEY

Job loss or financial constraints will soon be in your past, making way for a new, more prosperous time. Everything you went through was teaching you how to fail forward, take rejection as a learning point, and become stronger in your career. Accept that the end of the current cycle is clearing the way for even better financial or career opportunities.

PERSONAL/SPIRITUAL

After completing a painful cycle, you are moving forward with a new understanding of the past. You've cultivated gratitude for lessons learned and are starting a new chapter. Focus on overcoming stress and anxiety holistically through journaling or counseling. Continue on your healing journey through gentle healing modalities like acupuncture or Reiki.

REVERSED

The reversed Ten of Swords in your reading can signify a refusal to let something come to an end. Remind yourself that it is perfectly fine to let go and move on. Clinging to the past prevents the emergence of a new beginning. Try not to delay the abundance that awaits you.

REFLECT

→ What is the most challenging part of ending a cycle?

PAGE *of* SWORDS

The messenger of communication brings a fresh perspective; be open to hearing and sharing ideas.

Pages are the first of the four court cards and are considered the messengers of the tarot. The Page of Swords has a youthful energy and may represent a child or younger person, or even a message from your own inner child, urging you to follow your natural curiosity and be open to learning new things. The young Page of Swords stands with his sword raised, practicing for a battle that may arise. He wants to be prepared, feels excited and nervous, and appears to look around to see who is coming. Practicing how to wield his sword with intention builds his confidence, ensuring he will be ready to engage when the time is right.

UPRIGHT KEY MEANINGS

Enthusiasm, eagerness to learn

REVERSED KEY MEANINGS

Gossip, defensiveness

ELEMENTAL COMBINATION

Earth & air. Earth signifies the Page's connection to nature and stability, and his place in the suit of Swords connects him to air, which represents communication and wisdom.

GENERAL READING

The Page of Swords is grounded enough to know he must practice before leaping into conflict. This energy is urging you to pay attention to the subtle messages surrounding you, urging you to move forward but with measured caution. Communication, fresh perspectives, and opportunities to engage your mind surround you right now. You may be feeling apprehensive, but something is begging you to follow your enthusiasm. Creating a solid plan before you begin will help boost your confidence.

LOVE/ROMANCE

A partner with a quick, curious mind, possibly younger or with a youthful attitude, will arrive in your life soon. This person may also offer new perspectives that you hadn't previously considered. While you may be in a relationship filled with plenty of moments of lighthearted fun, there is also a need to share your truths with each other or to learn from one another.

CAREER/MONEY

You're waiting to hear back from a client, manager, or new employer—and this news will offer valuable information to new options or help you expand your horizons. This news may excite you, but be sure to formulate a solid plan before jumping in. Be confident in sharing your thoughts and ideas.

PERSONAL/SPIRITUAL

You're feeling excitement and curiosity about a new course of study or interest in your journey to enrich yourself physically, emotionally, mentally, or spiritually. In the process, you may unearth new truths about yourself.

REVERSED

The reversed Page of Swords in your reading can represent insidious gossip or manipulation tactics, perpetrated either by you or by someone around you. Bear in mind that the information you share with others may not be kept private, and notice how you feel when you're around people who are gossiping or talking about someone who isn't present.

REFLECT

→ What ideas could the Page of Swords be bringing to you right now?

KNIGHT *of* SWORDS

The quest for truth pushes you forward at all costs, and you plow ahead without considering the consequences.

Knights in the tarot are depicted on horseback, returning from a noble quest to present you with an elemental item that you requested. The Knight of Swords represents pure air and is depicted charging forward against the wind, brandishing his sword of truth. This Knight moves quickly, with his laser focus trained on the prize he seeks. The speed and aggressive body language suggest he is heading toward confrontation and drama, and that there is no stopping him.

UPRIGHT KEY MEANINGS
Truth seeking, assertive

REVERSED KEY MEANINGS
Pushy, aggressive

ELEMENTAL COMBINATION
Air & air. Air signifies the Knight's connection to communication and wisdom, and his place in the suit of Swords also connects him to air, which gives this Knight a double dose of clear insight and swift speech.

GENERAL READING

The Knight of Swords may represent a situation that must be dealt with head-on, indicating that confrontation cannot be avoided. Perhaps it is asking you to be more assertive or to focus on your goals with all of your available energy. This card may also point toward a person in your life who is trying to engage you in their drama. Your intuition will guide you toward who or what this swiftly moving energy represents in your life.

LOVE/ROMANCE

A potential romantic partner is coming on too strong, or someone is pursuing you too intensely. This may feel flattering or manic, depending on your own temperament, so listen to your intuition if this suitor makes you feel uneasy. This card may also represent a romance that starts out strong but fizzles out just as quickly.

CAREER/MONEY

Being more assertive and focused on a goal or project, or just applying yourself more intensely in general, will bring change at work. Potential drama with a boss or coworker may put you in a position where you must defend yourself in some way. News that is coming quickly will speed up productivity or cause you to shift your course of action.

PERSONAL/SPIRITUAL

You've been getting caught up in dramatic encounters and feeling defensive. Alternately, you're exploring a new, assertive side of your personality by pursuing a goal or idea with great focus and confidence. You can look forward to receiving news you have been waiting on and rest in the knowledge that you'll act accordingly.

REVERSED

The reversed Knight of Swords in your points to the aggressive side of ambition, possibly including pushing yourself or others to extremes. There is a possibility you might run out of steam and feel disappointed by something that started out strong and lost momentum. If this is true, take a step back to reflect and tune in to your intuition. Look within yourself to find a way back to productive action.

REFLECT ·················

→ How does the speed indicated on this card make you feel?

QUEEN *of* **SWORDS**

Feminine energy of protection, fairness, and balance when making decisions and speaking the truth is held within the Queen of Swords.

....

Queens in tarot represent feminine energy that includes receptivity, honesty, compassion, and love. The Queen of Swords represents the elements of water and air, yet there is very little water in the card itself, just a faraway stream. This indicates that clear communication, intellect, and logic are favored over emotional outpouring. This Queen is seated on a sturdy throne, welcoming anyone who seeks her counsel, yet she holds her sword of truth in front of her, making it clear that she will not hide her thoughts and opinions. This Queen is wise and just; her thoughtfully drawn conclusions are trusted by all who surround her. To remain in balance, she is open to hearing the opinions and ideas of others.

UPRIGHT KEY MEANINGS
Decisiveness, honesty

REVERSED KEY MEANINGS
Criticism, defensiveness

ELEMENTAL COMBINATION
Water & air. Water signifies the Queen's connection to love and emotion, and her place in the suit of Swords connects her to air, which represents communication and wisdom.

GENERAL READING

The Queen of Swords can represent an actual person who embodies these characteristics, including yourself, or the energetic presence of intellect and wisdom in your life, particularly as it relates to decision-making. This card asks you to approach complex situations by formulating a logical response instead of an emotional reaction. Use your intuition to guide you toward who or what this card represents in your own life.

LOVE/ROMANCE

Try taking a logical approach so you can see a situation clearly within your relationship. You may be involved with a partner who is intelligent and trustworthy, who chooses reason over emotion. This relationship could be with someone who has lost their partner or someone who is a single parent. On the other hand, this may be your time to remain single and focus on your relationship with yourself, especially if you have experienced difficulties in remaining autonomous within relationships. It's not forever, and you're learning important things about yourself to bring into your next relationship.

CAREER/MONEY

Seek advice from a trusted colleague or someone in your industry, and make sure you're taking a logical approach to your finances and goals. If an investor or contract presents itself to you, read the fine print and make your decisions based on facts instead of a grand vision.

PERSONAL/SPIRITUAL

Stand up for your beliefs, and don't shy away from sharing your wisdom with others. Focus on using logic and reason rather than relying on emotional expressions, but beware of coming off as harsh in your delivery.

REVERSED

The reversed Queen of Swords in your reading can indicate that you, or someone else, are being overly critical of a person or situation. Sometimes, this can point toward an abundance of self-criticism, so be on the alert for that. This reversal can also indicate reacting defensively when confronted or allowing emotions to prevail over reason.

REFLECT

→ What advice would you ask of the Queen of Swords?

KING *of* SWORDS

Authoritative, masculine energy of taking action from a place of logic and reason are upheld within the King of Swords.

Masters of their suit, kings represent stability, authority, and healthy masculine energy. The King of Swords represents the elements of fire and air, empowering him to take action from the higher mind and intellect. The King is seated on a concrete throne carved with butterflies symbolic of the element of air as well as the transformative process of fire. The sword he holds is slightly tilted, suggesting movement and readiness to take action at a moment's notice.

UPRIGHT KEY MEANINGS
Intellectual ambition, leadership

REVERSED KEY MEANINGS
Control, judgment

ELEMENTAL COMBINATION
Fire & air. Fire signifies the King's connection to passion, action, and leadership, and his place in the suit of Swords connects him to air, which represents communication and wisdom.

GENERAL READING

The King of Swords can represent you or another person who embodies the qualities of authority, intelligence, and use of logic to attain success. It can also represent the energy of a situation requiring you to take decisive action on your own behalf or to stand up for others who may not have the power to defend themselves. Listen to your intuition for messages that can guide you when it's time to take action. You are a powerful authority who wields substantial intelligence. Trust your voice.

LOVE/ROMANCE

A partner who is highly intelligent and successful will express themselves through charming communication rather than passionate emotions. Taking a mature, rational approach in romance will yield better results at this time.

CAREER/MONEY

You are taking logical action on your goals, which may lead to becoming your own boss, receiving a promotion, or taking on a leadership role. This card may also represent an authority figure in the workplace or signal that you yourself are respected and recognized for your contributions. Good news in legal matters may be on the way.

PERSONAL/SPIRITUAL

Have the confidence to be the authority of your life by taking action on your own behalf or standing up for your ideas. If you feel yourself faltering, seek out the advice of a professional about your health or other domestic situation.

REVERSED

The reversed King of Swords in your reading can indicate an overblown sense of intellectual superiority or acting in judgmental ways. You may be fighting against controlling behavior, yours or someone else's, which works directly against the flow of your intuition and divine timing. Let go of the need to control the details and actions of others to rebalance this energy.

REFLECT ·······························

→ How can you channel the ambitious energy of the King of Swords?

CHAPTER 8

Minor Arcana: Wands

....

THE WANDS REPRESENT the elemental suit of fire and the fire signs in astrology: Aries, Leo, and Sagittarius. Wands are symbolic of passion, creativity, ambition, and action. Beginning with the Ace of Wands, we will explore the universal meanings of each card. An easy way of remembering that wands are associated with creation, drive, and action is to think about the phrase "waving a magic wand" to make something appear instantly. Fire moves quickly and transforms every object it touches, just as a magician's wand triggers transformation through the power of intention. Remembering that wands are powerful tools of creation will help you learn about this suit quickly and easily.

....

ACE of WANDS

The gift of creation is presented from the divine. Be open to exciting new possibilities.

The Ace of Wands brings the gift of a new beginning rooted in passion and creativity. The hand of the divine emerges from a cloud, offering a single wand of visionary inspiration, sprouting green leaves. Beneath the wand is a lush landscape that includes a castle, a peaceful river, and a handful of fertile trees. This scene depicts stability, prosperity, movement, and the current of emotions that propels you forward, supporting a new venture.

UPRIGHT KEY MEANINGS

Inspiration, creativity

REVERSED KEY MEANINGS

Hesitation, delays

NUMEROLOGY

1, initiation, new beginning

GENERAL READING

When the Ace of Wands appears, it brings flashes of inspiration that guide you toward beginning a new adventure. This may manifest as creating a new project, traveling, beginning a new relationship, or starting a business. This exciting energy is merely the first step, offering the drive and motivation you need to get moving on your path. Stay open to signs from the universe and take action when they appear!

LOVE/ROMANCE

A new, exciting relationship that's filled with passion and intensity is blooming. Or, if you're already partnered, you may sense increased or reignited passion, possibly leading you toward starting a family or expanding your current one. An exciting opportunity, for yourself or within your romance, is on its way.

CAREER/MONEY

This card heralds an exciting, inspiring opportunity to expand your business or start a new endeavor. You've been feeling increased creative enthusiasm for your work, which is opening doors to new forms of wealth. Take action when you are intuitively prompted!

PERSONAL/SPIRITUAL

When travel and adventure opportunities present themselves, embrace them! Beginning a health or fitness routine will bring renewed confidence and excitement into your life. This is an ideal time to take action on goals or creative projects you've been thinking about, so stay open to divine inspiration.

REVERSED

The reversed Ace of Wands in your reading can point to hesitation around taking action, perhaps driven by fears about timing, failure, or getting out of your comfort zone. Acknowledge what is preventing you from being bold and decisive so you are able to confidently move forward. This reversal may also indicate delays beyond your control. Trust that these delays are part of your divine timing, and try to stay flexible and open!

REFLECT ·······························

→ What gift is being presented by the Ace of Wands?

TWO *of* WANDS

*A choice to expand your world awaits.
Do you stay with what you know or
choose the unknown adventure?*

The Two of Wands card is an invitation to ponder the future. A man looks out onto the vast expansive land from a position high up in his luxurious castle. He has already established his position of stability, and now he craves adventure. One wand is securely anchored to the castle walls, showing his efforts to build his fortune, while the other wand is held above his head. In his other hand he holds a globe, as if to say the world is in his hands. Where will he go next? The Two of Wands signals an opportunity to plan for the next exciting phase in an already rich and full life.

UPRIGHT KEY MEANINGS
Choice, future plans

REVERSED KEY MEANINGS
Impatience, lack of planning

NUMEROLOGY
2, choice, partnership

GENERAL READING

The Two of Wands offers possibilities around making plans for the future. The exciting energy of fire propels you forward, but beware of becoming impatient and taking action too soon. You may need to choose between accepting a new opportunity or remaining where you are, so listen to your intuition. The one that excites you the most may be worth any associated risks. A new partnership or supportive relationship may be presenting itself to help you navigate these changes you're experiencing. This person will help you grow in new, exciting ways.

LOVE/ROMANCE

Get ready for an exciting new relationship rooted in passion, filled with flirtation, and packed with fun activities. You might be making travel plans for a romantic trip. Much is in motion, possibly including planning for the future with your partner or considering a move. These decisions are life-altering ones, so follow your intuitive guidance.

CAREER/MONEY

A new opportunity for growth in your career is no accident, so take action if you feel excited and intuitively guided. A business partner or investor is coming in to help you grow your ideas and take your plans to the next level.

PERSONAL/SPIRITUAL

Weigh your options before making a big decision, and heed intuitive guidance in your decision-making process. You're making plans and taking your goals to the next level and phase of life, which is exciting! Your life continues to be enriched when you follow a spiritual path and explore new directions.

REVERSED

The reversed Two of Wands in your reading can indicate impatience and acting hastily from a place of overexcitement. If you move forward too quickly and something doesn't work out the way you expected, don't give up! Simply slow down and do more research. Cultivate a clear plan of action before you try again. This reversal may also point to waiting for someone else to make a move before you can take action. This situation may require you to take initiative, even if doing so feels uncomfortable.

REFLECT ·······················

→ What new adventure is calling to you?

THREE *of* WANDS

Adventure lies ahead of you! As you expand into a new role or identity, you have plenty of support.

Filled with ambition and excitement, you're ready to expand into the next phase of your adventure in the Three of Wands card. The man depicted in this card has his back turned, which means that, as the viewer, you see what he sees. He stands between two wands planted in the ground, while he holds the third for support. He gazes out toward ships on the water, indicating the expansive nature of his dealings and suggesting that he works well with a team. The support of others allows him to conserve his energy without burning out and positions him to direct his considerable prowess toward big-picture tasks.

UPRIGHT KEY MEANINGS

Expansion, growth

REVERSED KEY MEANINGS

Delays, disappointment

NUMEROLOGY

3, expansion, collaboration

GENERAL READING

The Three of Wands indicates that you are using your energy to work with others, delegating and sharing responsibilities that play to your strengths. There may be an element of waiting for the right opportunities to come to you, but in the meantime you are able to use your energy creatively and productively, allowing expanded prosperity to grow, with a possibility of traveling.

LOVE/ROMANCE

You've met someone exciting through friends or by participating in activities you are passionate about. This could be a time of making travel plans with your partner or meeting someone special while on vacation. Consider infusing more excitement, passion, and expansiveness into your current relationship by planning for the future, gathering with friends, or participating in a group activity.

CAREER/MONEY

Work is presenting you with exciting collaborative opportunities. You may consider hiring a team or new employee due to increased profits or scaling up if you own your own business. This card can also signify traveling for work or conducting business overseas.

PERSONAL/SPIRITUAL

Surrounding yourself with inspiring people will help you expand to the next level of personal growth. You are expanding your spiritual practice whether you have the support of a community or you are calling in new friendships. Consider making travel plans that will expand your horizons and inspire you.

REVERSED

The reversed Three of Wands in your reading can indicate delays in your plans or a disconnection from a relationship or group of friends. This may be frustrating and disappointing, but it is part of divine timing and an important part of your learning journey. This reversal may indicate that there is a better solution available to you that has yet to present itself. Remaining flexible and patient is what is required at this time.

REFLECT

→ What three components of success does each of the three wands represent to you?

FOUR of WANDS

Celebrate your achievements with the ones you love before pushing ahead to the next goal.

Enjoyment and celebration abound in the Four of Wands card. A beautiful floral canopy that resembles a traditional Jewish chuppah, signifying marriage, is being held up by four wands firmly rooted in the ground. The yellow background of the card indicates conscious awareness and joy, as the couple celebrates their union by waving floral bouquets in the air enthusiastically. They have made the choice to unite in commitment to creating something stable and long-lasting. Behind the couple stands a glorious castle with people dancing joyfully in a lush garden, celebrating their abundance and prosperity.

UPRIGHT KEY MEANINGS

Celebration, special events

REVERSED KEY MEANINGS

Returning to the joy of the present

NUMEROLOGY

4, stability, structure

GENERAL READING

The Four of Wands indicates an organized celebration, such as a wedding, anniversary, or graduation. Look to your own life and achievements. How can you celebrate your wins? The enthusiasm you have for your relationships and local community are also celebrated here. Make sure you are balancing your hard work and ongoing efforts with relaxation.

LOVE/ROMANCE

An engagement, wedding, or honeymoon are indicated by this celebratory card. You may find yourself in a new relationship with someone who is open to love and a deeper commitment. If you're already partnered, you are considering moving in with a partner, buying a home together, or putting down roots in some way. You're enjoying the moment and finding love in your present situation.

CAREER/MONEY

Completing a project or goal finds you celebrating your success. You're enjoying some well-deserved recognition for your hard work and enthusiasm in the workplace. This is an exciting time of creativity and progress in your career, so take a moment to celebrate yourself.

PERSONAL/SPIRITUAL

You're savoring the process of putting down roots, either buying or renovating a home, joining a group, or taking a relationship to the next level. Celebrate the joy and excitement of these milestone moments. Should the opportunity arise, go ahead and pour your excitement into a creative project. Spending time with family and friends, throwing a party, or taking a break to rejuvenate is beneficial for your spirit.

REVERSED

The reversed Four of Wands is similar to the upright interpretation but reflects a bit of resistance to indulging in celebration. If you are resistant to enjoying the fruits of your labor, ask yourself why. Consider the present moment, and find the joy that exists right now. Celebrate yourself in some small way to increase the flow of positive opportunities into your life.

REFLECT

→ What achievement are you most proud of, and how does it make you feel?

FIVE *of* WANDS

The difference between rivalry and healthy competition asks you to work with your ego in a productive way.

How will you handle the competitive, dynamic energy of the Five of Wands card? Here you see five young men engaging in a competition, banging their wands around playfully. No one appears to be angry or hurt; instead, the focus is on active rivalry between worthy opponents and how ego drives their actions. The bright blue color of the card suggests a willingness to seek clarity amidst the struggle, while the absence of background landscape scenery focuses attention on the urgency of action and alertness required in the moment.

UPRIGHT KEY MEANINGS
Competition, rivalry

REVERSED KEY MEANINGS
Exaggeration, finding a solution

NUMEROLOGY
5, conflict, competition

GENERAL READING

The Five of Wands often shows up when you are steeped in conflict or disagreement and asks you to consider how you handle yourself during these situations. It can also indicate competition between qualified parties all vying for the same position, such as applying for the same job. When dealing with others who have strong opinions, know that your point of view is also important and don't be afraid to ruffle a few feathers in your quest for a successful outcome.

LOVE/ROMANCE

You may feel inclined to date multiple people before committing to an exclusive relationship. However, this card may also indicate you're feeling overwhelmed by relationship drama or the opinions of others about your love life. Ask yourself what you're looking for from a relationship so you can cut out anything interfering with your desired outcome.

CAREER/MONEY

Struggles or arguments in the workplace, or rivalry with coworkers, are consuming you. Competition for a promotion, or to deliver results, may be the driving energy at work. Success is within your grasp, so take strategic action and try not get caught up in egocentric battles.

PERSONAL/SPIRITUAL

Annoying delays and circumstances beyond your control are asking you to slow down and pay attention to details. Try to keep your impatience in check. Taking on several creative projects or tasks at the same time will lead to the frustration of not finishing anything. Focus on one thing at a time and see it through to its completion before beginning anything new.

REVERSED

The reversed Five of Wands in your reading can point to a conflict being blown out of proportion or the details of an argument or story being exaggerated for dramatic effect. Stick to the facts in order to avoid further drama and conflict. It also may point to a resolution or agreement reached after an argument.

REFLECT

→ What is your relationship to competition?

SIX of WANDS

Your hard work is being rewarded. Revel in this victorious moment surrounded by those who support you.

....

After struggling your way through a period of competition and opposition, you emerge victoriously in the Six of Wands card. On this card, we see a young man on a white horse symbolizing purity, riding through a cheering crowd raising their five wands in his honor. The rider raises his sixth wand higher than the rest, and both he and the wand are adorned with laurel wreaths, symbolic of victory. The five others in the crowd around him are reminiscent of the five young men fighting in the Five of Wands card, but this time they're gathering to acknowledge the victor with their support.

UPRIGHT KEY MEANINGS
Victory, recognition

REVERSED KEY MEANINGS
Delayed success

NUMEROLOGY
6, balance, harmony

GENERAL READING

Known as the victory card, the Six of Wands brings good news, especially after a period of struggle. An important feature of this card is that it focuses on feeling proud of your accomplishments, acknowledging your success, and accepting praise from others without shame or downplaying your success. You've worked hard and you deserve recognition, so allow yourself to shine in this moment. Your enthusiasm has the ability to lift others up as well.

LOVE/ROMANCE

This card signals a strong relationship or "power couple." You are involved with a romantic partner who matches your enthusiasm, passion, and intensity, so enjoy this exciting and dynamic relationship. You might be enjoying victory and success in love after a period of sadness or heartbreak.

CAREER/MONEY

Recognition or promotion for your efforts at work is on the table. This may manifest as public recognition in your career. Prosperity and an increase in finances are percolating now, after a period of struggle. Your discipline and hard work are paying off, so enjoy this time!

PERSONAL/SPIRITUAL

You are leveling up in all areas of life, enjoying your success, and being recognized for the wonderful work you do. Good news is coming to you related to your home or personal life. You're feeling ready to take on a leadership role within your community or special interest group.

REVERSED

The reversed Six of Wands in your reading can indicate a delay to your success in some way or events not turning out the way you'd anticipated. This is disappointing, but only a temporary setback. The delay is all part of the process, so stick with your plan and continue to work diligently. You're almost there; don't give up now.

REFLECT ······························

→ What success would you like to celebrate right now?

SEVEN *of* WANDS

Taking a stand for your beliefs is a necessary part of asserting yourself in the pursuit of your goals. You can handle whatever life throws at you.

Prepare to leap to the defense of your position with the Seven of Wands card. You'll see a young man using his wand as a weapon to defend himself against the six wands coming at him. He appears to have been taken by surprise, as he is wearing two different shoes! The rise to success is an entirely different journey than the one that begins once you've reached a goal and inspired envy in others. The identity of this man's attackers is a mystery, representing hidden challenges that inevitably arise and must be dealt with. How you address these obstacles and opponents determines which new levels of success will soon be within your grasp.

UPRIGHT KEY MEANINGS
Defensiveness, assertiveness

REVERSED KEY MEANINGS
Hypervigilance, feeling defeated

NUMEROLOGY
7, strategy, planning

GENERAL READING

The Seven of Wands deals with unforeseen challenges and obstacles that arise on your path, asking you to be assertive and strategic rather than acting defensive of your hard work and reputation. Being courageous in the face of adversity and listening to your intuition is the best way to handle pressure and increase your success.

LOVE/ROMANCE

Conflict resolution is a delicate dance, but don't hesitate to speak up for your needs, and be willing to hear your partner's. Relationship challenges may be present, but they can be overcome. Do not be afraid to meet difficulties in love. Instead, assert yourself and make your boundaries and intentions clear.

CAREER/MONEY

Negotiations for a raise or contract can reach a successful agreement; however, it is important to stand up for yourself and be assertive. Opposition or challenges may arise in your career, but they are temporary. You can still rise above this conflict and achieve your goals.

PERSONAL/SPIRITUAL

Momentary challenges are inviting you to be more assertive and courageous in your personal life. You may find yourself speaking on behalf of others or coming to the defense of a friend or family member. Maintain an objective stance, focus on the facts, and work toward a solution. Focusing on the problem will only cause you to stall out.

REVERSED

The reversed Seven of Wands can suggest you're letting your anger get the best of you by acting defensive and hypervigilant about your beliefs when challenged. It can also point to feeling defeated, as though standing up for yourself is pointless. Instead of lashing out when provoked, you may tend to internalize your anger and frustration. If this is the case, consider journaling about your feelings and then having a conversation, after you've had a chance to calm down and assess the situation. Your emotions are valid and deserve to be expressed.

REFLECT

→ What do you suppose the young man in the Seven of Wands is defending?

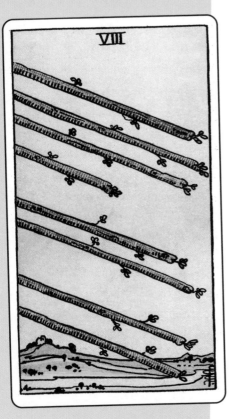

EIGHT of WANDS

Incoming news sparks a series of events that change your trajectory. You find yourself where you need to be and in the company of the right people. Flow with the current.

The Eight of Wands card brims with the energy of hastiness and speed. Along with the Aces and the Three of Swords, it is one of the only Minor Arcana cards that does not depict people. This puts an emphasis on the action taking place. Here you see eight budding wands flying through the air over a lovely pastoral landscape. These wands carry messages and can come in the form of letters, phone calls, emails, texts, or news heard from the lips of a passing stranger. However these messages come, they bring an element of excitement, speeding up events in your life and disrupting your daily routine, often in an overwhelmingly positive way!

UPRIGHT KEY MEANINGS
Movement, quick action

REVERSED KEY MEANINGS
Slowing down, exercising patience

NUMEROLOGY
8, movement, transition

GENERAL READING

There is an element of spontaneity in the Eight of Wands that gets you excited for an event that's on the verge of happening. This may involve travel or a new person coming into your life. Events move quickly, and everything falls into place without you needing to push for a particular outcome. Relax and ride the wave of excitement.

LOVE/ROMANCE

A new romantic partner may be about to enter your life through a series of seemingly random events. You may be feeling excitement around invitations to events, or being asked out by several people at once. If travel is in your future, it will be to see a partner.

CAREER/MONEY

One or multiple offers or ideas are coming to you, so get excited, but take your time deciding which ones to choose. Everything is speeding up in your career, moving you toward exciting new opportunities. You're drawing income from multiple sources and should remain open to receiving abundance in many ways!

PERSONAL/SPIRITUAL

You've got a jam-packed social schedule and are busily meeting new people and having fun. Life is moving you very quickly toward your personal goals, so go with the flow and you'll have the energy you need to take on whatever life has to offer. You may soon be traveling somewhere exciting, perhaps on a spontaneous trip.

REVERSED

The reversed Eight of Wands can indicate delays or hang-ups, which put a damper on your enthusiasm about something you'd been anticipating. These delays are no accident! They are divinely timed to highlight an important realization, something you need to recognize before you can continue down your current path. Perhaps this lack of movement is reminding you to enjoy the process without being so focused on the outcome.

REFLECT

→ Who do you think is sending out the Eight of Wands? Who might be receiving them?

NINE *of* WANDS

Despite the setbacks and struggles, you've come a long way. The end is in sight, so don't give up now.

The Nine of Wands card appears when you feel resolved but also a little exhausted by your journey. Eight wands stand tall in the ground as a weary man leans upon the ninth wand for support nearby. His head is bandaged, and he appears to have been through quite an ordeal. He takes a break to relive memories of the events that have led him to this point, knowing he has one last leg of the adventure to finish before he can relax fully.

UPRIGHT KEY MEANINGS
Persistence, self-reliance

REVERSED KEY MEANINGS
Giving up, delays

NUMEROLOGY
9, nearing completion, solitude

GENERAL READING

The Nine of Wands encompasses all of the events, struggles, and triumphs you've been dealing with up until this point. You may be exhausted and feel ready to give up—but you're almost there! It's time to dig deep into your reserves and push forward in the last stretch to complete your tasks. You are incredibly resilient, and you can handle any challenge that comes your way.

LOVE/ROMANCE

You've been dealing with difficulties that have prevented you from experiencing romantic fulfillment. Maybe you've been feeling alone in your relationship, work has kept you too busy to begin dating, or you're still healing from a prior relationship. Whatever it may be, the worst has passed and you're almost on the other side of these challenges.

CAREER/MONEY

Continue to persist in the pursuit of your goals. This current cycle of conflict is coming to an end, so don't give up. It's time to take the final steps toward finishing a project or wrapping up a long-term endeavor.

Pull from your energetic reserves to finish strong, and your hard work will pay off.

PERSONAL/SPIRITUAL

Trials and obstacles have taught you how self-reliant and resilient you are, especially in personal matters. Turning to your spiritual or wellness practice will help you reflect on these experiences to see the hidden gifts within each lesson. You're coming to the end of a struggle or conflict, so trust this process.

REVERSED

The reversed Nine of Wands can suggest you are ready to give up on something right before you reach your goal. The divine is urging you not to throw in the towel, no matter how oppressive the odds may seem. This reversal may also point to acting stubborn or getting in your own way somehow, preventing a cycle from completing. Even if another person appears to be the problem, remember that you can only control yourself. Gently observe your reactions and be willing to take responsibility for your behavior.

REFLECT ··

→ What story would the figure in the Nine of Wands be telling you about his experiences?

TEN of WANDS

Be mindful of taking on too many responsibilities. It is perfectly reasonable to protect your energy and say "no."

....

After digging into your energetic reserves for a long-haul effort, you find yourself pushed past your limits in the Ten of Wands card. A man struggles to carry a bundle of ten wands, representing the difficult task of juggling multiple areas of life at once. He makes his way toward a beautiful house in the distance, but his head is down; the wands are heavy and obstructing his view. He appears to trudge blindly forward, pushing himself to his physical limits. The blue color of the card represents mental clarity, indicating the man knows he must complete this task no matter how uncomfortable and stressful it feels in the moment. Peace of mind is just on the other side of this experience.

UPRIGHT KEY MEANINGS
Overwhelm, burdens

REVERSED KEY MEANINGS
Pressure, exhaustion

NUMEROLOGY
10, complete cycle

GENERAL READING

The Ten of Wands tells of the burdens of responsibility we carry, and it signals being completely overwhelmed by taking on too many tasks. Living at this level of action takes its toll on your body, nervous system, and emotions, leaving nothing for yourself or the people you love. Consider your motivations; why are you driving yourself so hard? Learning to ask for help or delegate responsibility frees you up to put better-quality energy into the things that light you up the most.

LOVE/ROMANCE

Taking on too many responsibilities may be leaving you with no personal downtime, let alone time to meet new people. It may be taking a toll on your relationship, and this card is asking you to make more time for romance. Perhaps you are carrying all of the responsibility and duties within a relationship and feeling worn out. A partner may be putting too much pressure on you, relying on you for emotional and/or financial support.

CAREER/MONEY

You have been taking on too many tasks at work and are experiencing burnout. Ask for help without doubting your abilities, and establish boundaries so you are not working around the clock. Since you are reaching the end of a big project or assignment that has stretched you to your limits, you'll be able to rest soon.

PERSONAL/SPIRITUAL

Saying yes to everything and everyone has left you feeling burned-out and overburdened. Creating boundaries and saying no can feel uncomfortable in the moment, but it is much more sustainable than taking on the weight of the world. You may be taking on incredible amounts of responsibility or creative projects in order to meet your personal goals.

REVERSED

The reversed Ten of Wands in your reading can indicate putting tremendous pressure on yourself to succeed or having perfectionist tendencies that lead to extreme exhaustion and burnout. Try to take on only what you can handle without judging your productivity or comparing yourself to others. Balance activities that bring you joy with those that must be done, and say "no" to the rest.

REFLECT

→ Where have you been taking on too many responsibilities?

PAGE_of WANDS.

PAGE *of* WANDS

The messenger of fire brings exciting news.
Be open to adventurous opportunities.

....

The Page of Wands is full of youthful energy
and may represent a child or younger person
or even a message from your own inner
child, urging you to be more playful and
adventurous. The young Page stands still,
gazing at his wand as if he is imagining
its endless uses. It is unusual to see him in
motionless contemplation, a posture that
reveals his connection to the earth element.
He is both grounded and curious, a combination that allows him to play without
getting hurt, as noted on his tunic by the
salamanders—creatures with fireproof skin.

UPRIGHT KEY MEANINGS

Impulsiveness, sense
of adventure

....

REVERSED KEY MEANINGS

Unreliability, hastiness

....

ELEMENTAL KEY
COMBINATION

Earth & fire. Earth signifies the
Page's connection to nature
and stability, and his place in
the suit of Wands connects
him to fire, which represents
passion and action.

GENERAL READING

The Page of Wands is grounded yet playful, someone who sees the world through a lens of curiosity. Good news, possibly through email, texts, phone calls, or direct conversations, is coming your way. Be open to creative experiences, new opportunities, and expressing yourself in ways that feel fresh and dynamic.

LOVE/ROMANCE

You are drawn to a romantic partner who is fun and outgoing, talkative, and ready to have adventures, although this person may lack follow-through on their grandiose promises. Actions speak louder than words. Carving out time for playful activities in your existing relationship will bring you closer together.

CAREER/MONEY

A job offer or opportunity is coming that will excite you and reignite your passion for what you do. You've been feeling very busy and needing to prioritize your tasks, so implement time-management practices in order to stay on top of your work. Make sure you can deliver on your promises.

PERSONAL/SPIRITUAL

An exciting time of new beginnings is on its way, but it will require a grounded approach. Try not to overcommit yourself; take a pause before responding and make sure you have the time and energy to follow through on your agreements. Get in touch with your inner child by revisiting the activities you loved when you were young. Spending time with actual children can also be very healing for you.

REVERSED

The reversed Page of Wands in your reading can indicate taking hasty, impulsive actions before having a proper plan in place. This leads to letting yourself and others down, giving you or someone else a reputation of unreliability. Everyone does this from time to time! Take on only what you know you'll have the energy to complete. This may relate to a child in your life or someone acting childish, complaining about their responsibilities rather than addressing the task at hand.

REFLECT ••

→ What do you think the Page of Wands is about to get into?

KNIGHT *of* WANDS.

KNIGHT *of* WANDS

The quest for action drives this Knight to swoop in and take the lead, delivering swift results.

Knights in the tarot are depicted on horseback, returning from a noble quest to present you with an elemental item that you requested. On the Knight of Wands card, the combination of air and fire ignites a flame to blazing proportions, propelling him to take bold action without fear of getting hurt. The salamanders on his tunic, symbolic of this creature's fireproof skin, protect the Knight of Wands in addition to the armor he wears. He rides swiftly across a barren landscape, holding a budding wand, symbolic of new ideas and growth. This Knight is passionate and brave, and puts words into action to get the job done. Sometimes he may be a little too ambitious and hasty, but usually his success is ensured.

UPRIGHT KEY MEANINGS

Fast action, passion

REVERSED KEY MEANINGS

Self-doubt, hesitation

ELEMENTAL KEY COMBINATION

Air & fire. Air signifies the Knight's connection to communication, while his place in the suit of Wands connects him to fire, which represents passion and action.

GENERAL READING

The Knight of Wands indicates the time has arrived to take action on your ideas or projects. Consider this the green light to begin! Once you take the first step, notice how everything else begins to speed up to propel you in the direction you have chosen. Have confidence in yourself or in others who have come to support you. If you have been feeling blocked or stagnant, this energy comes to reignite the spark of passion and move you along the path toward your goals. Pay attention to your intuitive urges and act on them without hesitation.

LOVE/ROMANCE

A charming, passionate partner might be very active in pursuing you. A new relationship is moving extremely fast, but try to enjoy the moment without getting too carried away, since this type of pace is not sustainable in the long run. You may meet someone while traveling, or find that traveling with your current partner rekindles the spark between you.

CAREER/MONEY

Business is picking up quickly. Following your intuition in business leads to increased profits, or your instincts may lead to the next action steps that move you toward success. You're enjoying progress after a period of stagnation, so take action when prompted. A new project, possibly creative in nature, will spark your enthusiasm and get you motivated.

PERSONAL/SPIRITUAL

You're busily enjoying movement and action on your goals, possibly moving house. Good news and support are on their way to help you make progress if you have been delayed or feeling stuck in a situation. Your enthusiasm for life in general is finally returning, giving you increased energy to apply to your passions.

REVERSED

The reversed Knight of Wands in your reading can indicate self-doubt in a general sense, but most likely related to a specific goal or situation that hasn't progressed in the way you'd hoped. Delays and misunderstandings are part of life, not a sign to give up. There may be a different and better course of action to take, so have patience and make use of this time by tuning into your intuition for guidance.

REFLECT ·····································

→ What would you like the Knight of Wands to bring you?

QUEEN of WANDS

Feminine energy of intuitive creativity and emotional intelligence combined with passion and heart-centered action are held within the Queen of Wands.

In tarot, queens represent feminine energy that includes receptivity, creativity, nurturing, and love. The addition of the fire element combined with intuitive water gives this Queen action-driven capabilities for giving as well as receiving. The Queen of Wands is seated facing the viewer, displaying confidence rather than passivity. Her gaze is to the left, the direction of intuition, symbolic of her connection to water and feminine energy. This powerful combination is much like that of the Magician, who channels the divine to manifest his reality, and the Queen of Wands has been historically referred to as "the witch of the tarot" for this reason. In this case, the term "witch" refers to her ability to manifest and is not connected to a specific religion. The black cat by her side, known as the witch's familiar, echoes this aptly given nickname.

UPRIGHT KEY MEANINGS
Creativity, ambition

REVERSED KEY MEANINGS
Feeling unworthy, creative blocks

ELEMENTAL KEY COMBINATION
Water & fire. Water signifies the Queen's connection to love and emotions, while her place in the suit of Wands connects her to fire, which represents passion and action.

GENERAL READING

The Queen of Wands indicates an invitation to step fully into your own power, own your ambition, and allow yourself to take on leadership opportunities. As you claim your power, know that you are guided and protected now and always. Your confidence and sense of worthiness are elevated, and your reality will rise to match your energy.

LOVE/ROMANCE

You are drawn to a strong, confident, and compassionate partner. They are established and successful, and this is exciting and perhaps intimidating. Know that you are equally matched energetically, and enjoy this connection. By owning your power within your relationship, you find that you are stronger than you think.

CAREER/MONEY

You're feeling powerful and enjoying being recognized in the workplace. If you are an entrepreneur or owner, listen to your intuition to grow your business and take action toward increased prosperity. Your creativity and enthusiasm are an important part of your success, for yourself and in the ways you inspire others. Consider taking a leadership position or speaking engagement if one presents itself.

PERSONAL/SPIRITUAL

Focus on cultivating your intuitive powers within your spiritual practice and manifesting your dreams into reality. This may mean spending time in nature to rejuvenate your energy and spirit before returning to your responsibilities. Take initiative to work on healing any blocks to your self-esteem and sense of self-worth. You are becoming more confident, which will lead to immense personal growth and improved relationships.

REVERSED

The reversed Queen of Wands in your reading can indicate doubting your value or worthiness, or feeling as though others do not recognize these qualities within you. Once you begin to cultivate belief in yourself, you'll start to see a shift in your confidence that empowers you to take action on your own behalf. Others will recognize this transformation and approach you with more respect and admiration.

REFLECT ••

→ What do you want to create by harnessing the passionate energy of the Queen of Wands?

KING of WANDS

Healthy masculine energy of confidence, loyalty, and leadership while taking action from a place of stability and integrity are upheld within the King of Wands.

In tarot, kings are the masters of their suit, representing stability, authority, and healthy masculine energy. The King of Wands represents the double element of fire, symbolizing pure ambition and action. The King is seated on his throne featuring lions and salamanders, symbolic of strength and protection. Looking off into the distance, he appears ready to jump into action at any moment, with a live salamander at his side to join him if necessary. Although the King of Wands has experienced plenty of activity, he knows how to delegate tasks and reserve his energy.

UPRIGHT KEY MEANINGS
Power, authority

REVERSED KEY MEANINGS
Abuse of power, bullying

ELEMENTAL KEY COMBINATION
Fire & fire. Fire signifies the King's connection to passion, action, and leadership, while his place in the suit of Wands connects him to fire, offering a double dose of passionate leadership in action.

GENERAL READING

The King of Wands may represent a person who embodies the qualities of leadership, authority, stability, and calm in the face of adversity, or this card may be asking that you step into an authoritative role in some area of your life. By relying on your instincts with maturity and confidence, you can take decisive action with enthusiasm. Notice how you react around others who display these characteristics.

LOVE/ROMANCE

You've been charmed by a charismatic partner who embodies the qualities of stability, authority, and success. The two of you may be destined for a mature relationship based on loyalty, taking action, and stability. There is strong passion and desire between you and your partner, but beware of egos clashing. If you are both trying to take the lead, compromise is necessary.

CAREER/MONEY

This card shows you as an entrepreneur, or taking initiative and making the first moves toward a goal. You may find yourself leading a team and having support in the workplace. Remain true to your natural integrity, since many people trust your strength and skills. This card indicates you are making tremendous progress in your career or leveling up/scaling a business.

PERSONAL/SPIRITUAL

You're entering a period of taking action based on your intuition and confidently asserting yourself. This may involve travel, perhaps on your own. You're working hard on mastering your responses and reactions to others without losing your cool. It may mean you are feeling more confident in your talents and craft.

REVERSED

The reversed King of Wands can point to unhealthy displays of masculine energy such as abuse of power in a situation, holding grudges, or acting like a bully. Healthy masculine energy understands the responsibility that comes with being in a place of power and seeks to empower others to act with integrity. Tune into your intuition to see where this selfish or oppressive energy may be coming from.

REFLECT

→ What in your life requires your action and attention?

Quick Reference Guide

Major Arcana

PAGE	CARD		UPRIGHT MEANING	REVERSED MEANING
54	THE FOOL		New beginning, freedom	Naiveté, fear of change
56	THE MAGICIAN		Manifestation, creator, inspired action	Disconnection from personal power, manipulative
58	THE HIGH PRIESTESS		Intuition, self-knowledge	Disconnection from intuition, refusal to look within
60	THE EMPRESS		Receiving love, creativity	Disconnection, creative blocks
62	THE EMPEROR		Inspired action, personal power	Inability to take action, or defensive/reactive
64	THE HIEROPHANT		Teacher, tradition	Rigid beliefs, refusal to learn

PAGE	CARD		UPRIGHT MEANING	REVERSED MEANING
66	THE LOVERS		Relationship, alignment	Disharmony, imbalance
68	THE CHARIOT		Inspired action, momentum	Inability to move forward, stagnation
70	STRENGTH		Overcoming obstacles, endurance	Apprehension, lacking confidence
72	THE HERMIT		Wisdom, solitude	Loneliness, isolation
74	WHEEL OF FORTUNE		Cycles, change	Delays, setbacks
76	JUSTICE		Truth, balance	Imbalance, unfair treatment

Major Arcana (cont.)

PAGE	CARD	UPRIGHT MEANING	REVERSED MEANING
78	THE HANGED MAN	Waiting, shifting perspective	Impatience, inertia
80	DEATH	Transformation, release	Clinging to the past, refusing to change
82	TEMPERANCE	Moderation, harmony, divine timing	Imbalance, pushing for results
84	THE DEVIL	Sabotage, addiction	Release, liberation
86	THE TOWER	Upheaval, sudden change	Hanging on, fear of letting go

PAGE	CARD		UPRIGHT MEANING	REVERSED MEANING
88	THE STAR		Hope, healing	Loss of faith, disconnection from source
90	THE MOON		Dreams, illusions	Bypassing difficulties, refusing to acknowledge the truth
92	THE SUN		Clarity, optimism	Pessimism, confusion
94	JUDGMENT		Awakening, acceptance	Self-doubt, resentment
96	THE WORLD		Successful completion, reaping rewards	Incomplete action, delayed celebration

Minor Arcana: Cups

PAGE	CARD		UPRIGHT MEANING	REVERSED MEANING
100	ACE OF CUPS		New love, relationships	Depletion, disappointment
102	TWO OF CUPS		Partnership, union	Disharmony, breakup
104	THREE OF CUPS		Celebration, togetherness	Feeling emotionally drained, overindulgence
106	FOUR OF CUPS		Apathy, stagnation	Refusal to change, stuck in a bad mood
108	FIVE OF CUPS		Grief, sadness	Silver linings, moving on
110	SIX OF CUPS		Harmony, memories	Nostalgia, living in the past

PAGE	CARD		UPRIGHT MEANING	REVERSED MEANING
112	SEVEN OF CUPS		Possibilities, daydreaming	Illusions, confusion
114	EIGHT OF CUPS		Walking away, moving on	Hanging on, avoiding change
116	NINE OF CUPS		Satisfaction, abundance	Overindulgence, arrogance
118	TEN OF CUPS		Happiness, fulfillment	Disharmony
120	PAGE OF CUPS		Love messages, playfulness, emotional intelligence	Immaturity, oversensitivity
122	KNIGHT OF CUPS		Emotional offerings, speed	Perfectionism, disappointment

Minor Arcana: Cups (cont.)

PAGE	CARD		UPRIGHT MEANING	REVERSED MEANING
124	QUEEN OF CUPS		Nurturing, feminine energy	Suspicion, emotional distance
126	KING OF CUPS		Emotional stability, empathy	Unreliability, lack of boundaries

Minor Arcana: Pentacles

PAGE	CARD		UPRIGHT MEANING	REVERSED MEANING
130	ACE OF PENTACLES		New beginnings, abundance	Delayed abundance
132	TWO OF PENTACLES		Balance, stability	Tension, irresponsibility
134	THREE OF PENTACLES		Success, new doors opening	Burnout, lack of confidence

PAGE	CARD		UPRIGHT MEANING	REVERSED MEANING
136	FOUR OF PENTACLES		Building stability, conserving resources	Materialism, controlling behaviors
138	FIVE OF PENTACLES		Focusing on lack, feeling physically or financially depleted	Moving on from challenges
140	SIX OF PENTACLES		Generosity, sharing resources	Generosity with strings attached, inequality
142	SEVEN OF PENTACLES		Growth, patience	Impatience, procrastination
144	EIGHT OF PENTACLES		Hard work, productivity	Burnout, overworking, being undervalued
146	NINE OF PENTACLES		Success, enjoyment	Materialism, lack of appreciation

Minor Arcana: Pentacles (cont.)

PAGE	CARD		UPRIGHT MEANING	REVERSED MEANING
148	TEN OF PENTACLES		Wealth, family, inheritance	Loss, breaking with tradition
150	PAGE OF PENTACLES		Manifestation, solid beginnings	Procrastination, lacking a solid plan
152	KNIGHT OF PENTACLES		Long-term abundance, steady progress	Hesitation, complacency
154	QUEEN OF PENTACLES		Generosity, dependability	Materialism, unreliability
156	KING OF PENTACLES		Wealth, generosity	Greed, self-centeredness

Minor Arcana: Swords

PAGE	CARD		UPRIGHT MEANING	REVERSED MEANING
160	ACE OF SWORDS		Clarity, new ideas	Confusion, indecision
162	TWO OF SWORDS		Indecision, self-protection	Manipulation, blocked intuition
164	THREE OF SWORDS		Sadness, pain	Recovery, releasing pain
166	FOUR OF SWORDS		Rest, introspection	Restlessness, avoiding self-reflection
168	FIVE OF SWORDS		Conflict, arguments	Releasing, letting go of grudges
170	SIX OF SWORDS		Moving forward, embarking on a healing journey	Difficulties in moving on, staying in place

Minor Arcana: Swords (cont.)

PAGE	CARD		UPRIGHT MEANING	REVERSED MEANING
172	SEVEN OF SWORDS		Deception, strategy	Disorganization, paranoia
174	EIGHT OF SWORDS		Feeling trapped, restriction	Release, hesitation
176	NINE OF SWORDS		Anxiety, worry	Hopelessness, despair
178	TEN OF SWORDS		Endings, new beginnings	Delayed endings, hanging on to the past
180	PAGE OF SWORDS		Enthusiasm, eagerness to learn	Gossip, defensiveness
182	KNIGHT OF SWORDS		Truth seeking, assertive	Pushy, aggressive

PAGE	CARD		UPRIGHT MEANING	REVERSED MEANING
184	QUEEN OF SWORDS		Decisiveness, honesty	Criticism, defensiveness
186	KING OF SWORDS		Intellectual ambition, leadership	Control, judgment

Minor Arcana: Wands

PAGE	CARD		UPRIGHT MEANING	REVERSED MEANING
190	ACE OF WANDS		Inspiration, creativity	Hesitation, delays
192	TWO OF WANDS		Choice, future plans	Impatience, lack of planning
194	THREE OF WANDS		Expansion, growth	Delays, disappointment

Minor Arcana: Wands (cont.)

PAGE	CARD		UPRIGHT MEANING	REVERSED MEANING
196	FOUR OF WANDS		Celebration, special events	Returning to the joy of the present
198	FIVE OF WANDS		Competition, rivalry	Exaggeration, finding a solution
200	SIX OF WANDS		Victory, recognition	Delayed success
202	SEVEN OF WANDS		Defensiveness, assertiveness	Hypervigilance, feeling defeated
204	EIGHT OF WANDS		Movement, quick action	Slowing down, exercising patience
206	NINE OF WANDS		Persistence, self-reliance	Giving up, delays

PAGE	CARD		UPRIGHT MEANING	REVERSED MEANING
208	TEN OF WANDS		Overwhelm, burdens	Pressure, exhaustion
210	PAGE OF WANDS		Impulsiveness, sense of adventure	Unreliability, hastiness
212	KNIGHT OF WANDS		Fast action, passion	Self-doubt, hesitation
214	QUEEN OF WANDS		Creativity, ambition	Feeling unworthy, creative blocks
216	KING OF WANDS		Power, authority	Abuse of power, bullying

Resources

....

I'VE COMPILED A handy list of books, tarot decks, shops, and websites that are great for beginners seeking to continue their tarot journey through interactive, experiential practice. These classic books reside in my personal library and have taught me a great deal over the years. While my first tarot deck was a copy of the classic Rider Waite Smith used in this book, I've also highlighted a few of my favorite modern decks. These decks feature diversity and inclusivity and focus on developing intuition rather than upholding tradition, offering new perspectives through the interpretive lens of the artist. Blending traditional wisdom with contemporary experience has expanded my personal practice, and I'm excited to share my resources with you.

....

Tarot Books

21 WAYS TO READ A TAROT CARD by Mary K. Greer

www.marykgreer.com

A fantastic interactive approach to reading tarot that focuses on both traditional and personal interpretations. Greer uses a variety of outside-the-box methods to connect with your deck and expand your practice.

TAROT WISDOM: SPIRITUAL TEACHINGS AND DEEPER MEANINGS by Rachel Pollack

www.rachelpollack.com

An in-depth look at several classic and modern tarot decks' artwork, interpretations, and personal stories from one of the most respected voices in tarot. Pollack's book *78 Degrees of Wisdom* is considered the "tarot bible" by many and also makes an excellent reference book. This book, however, includes numerous insightful tarot spreads and focuses on the storytelling aspect of tarot. I highly recommend both.

THE TAROT: HISTORY, SYMBOLISM, AND DIVINATION by Robert Place

www.robertmplacetarot.com

A thorough and in-depth history of tarot's origins, this book focuses on the many mystical symbols in each tarot card and offers information on their full esoteric meanings. Place combines his attention to historical accuracy with his own intuitive insight, offering his signature methods of three-card spread readings.

Tarot Decks

THE MOON VOID TAROT by Stefanie Caponi

www.moonvoidtarot.com

A contemporary deck featuring black-and-white artwork that follows one central character's journey through the tarot, this is a perfect deck for shadow work and self-reflection. The guidebook puts an emphasis on combining tarot and astrology, offering several unique tarot spreads.

THE MODERN WITCH TAROT DECK by Lisa Sterle

www.lisasterle.com

This contemporary spin on Rider Waite Smith imagery features refreshing diversity and an all-female/femme/fluid cast of characters, embodying the classic archetypes in modern, relatable settings.

THE WILD UNKNOWN TAROT by Kim Krans

www.thewildunknown.com

A new classic emphasizing nature and featuring animals rather than humans. This beautifully illustrated deck and guidebook feature simple interpretations, placing the focus on the elements and nature.

SOUL CARDS TAROT by Kristine Fredheim

www.soulcardstarot.com

This beautiful minimalist tarot deck is a contemporary take on the Marseille Tarot, featuring gorgeous abstract graphics without any people. It is available in blush pink or midnight black.

Stores & Online Shops

CATLAND BOOKS

www.catlandbooks.com

Brooklyn's premier occult bookstore and apothecary. Shop their entire catalog of tarot decks, specialty books, and independent zines not found anywhere else.

HAUS WITCH

www.hauswitch.com

Salem's popular outpost, carrying everything from tarot decks to contemporary home decor that will infuse magic into every corner of your home.

LITTLE RED TAROT

www.littleredtarot.com

UK-based online retailer and long-running blog featuring insightful posts on a broad range of tarot topics in addition to stocking an impressive collection of indie tarot and oracle decks for overseas shoppers.

PHOENIX & LOTUS

www.phoenix-lotus.com

Online retailer focused on independent designers, offering a wonderfully curated selection of indie tarot and oracle decks.

Acknowledgments

....

I'D LIKE TO express my gratitude to Robie Evangelista for opening the doors of possibility with an act of generosity; to my incredible editors, Meg Ilasco and Sally McGraw, and the team at Penguin Random House who brought this project together and taught me so much; and to my coven of tarot witches, who have shown me the true meaning of friendship and magical community.

....

About the Author

STEFANIE CAPONI (SHE/HER) is an intuitive writer and illustrator. She has been reading tarot for more than 20 years and established her business as a professional tarot reader after creating her first tarot deck, *The Moon Void Tarot*. Her work is centered on exploring shadow work, healing, and creativity using tarot as a vehicle to access the hidden realms of the self. In addition to her work with tarot, she also writes monthly horoscopes for Dame Products. Connect with Stefanie on Instagram **@moonvoidtarot** and at **moonvoidtarot.com**.

Embrace the timeless teachings of the chakra system for peace of mind, better physical health, and a sense of alignment, fulfillment, and purpose with Reiki master and wellness expert Ambi Kavanagh.

"*Chakras & Self-Care* is a perfect balance of precision and tenderness . . . Ambi Kavanagh's approach reinvigorated my understanding and rebooted my practice." —Erica Chidi, cofounder and CEO, LOOM

Featuring more than 100 spells, rituals, and potion recipes, this practical grimoire helps witches of all skill levels amplify healing for an invigorating life and an enriched world.

"*The Healing Power of Witchcraft* is packed with smart spells and rituals for all kinds of healings. This book is sure to inspire readers to feel more whole, capable, and empowered to create positive changes in their lives." —Astrea Taylor, author of *Intuitive Witchcraft*

Crystal healer and Reiki master Mariah K. Lyons shares her knowledge in this beautifully illustrated, practical guide for crystal healing that helps womxn awaken feminine divinity and healing powers and rekindle their instinctual relationship with nature.

"*Crystal Healing for Women* is a lucid guide to the glistening world of gems. Mariah leads us through rituals and practices that activate our relationship to Earth's most mystical stones." —Kim Krans, *New York Times* bestselling author

zeitgeistpublishing.com